The Evolution
of Modern Sailboat Design

The Evolution
of Modern Sailboat Design

Meade Gougeon
Ty Knoy

Illustrations by Leon C. Stecker

WINCHESTER PRESS

Library of Congress Catalog Card Number: 73-75666
ISBN 0-87691-098-3

Published by Winchester Press
460 Park Avenue, New York 10022

Printed in the United States of America

Contents

Introduction *vii*

I   Early Developments in Rigs and Hulls **1**

II   Less Weight and More Speed **23**

III   Sailboats for Pleasure **43**

IV   Small Boats and New Ideas **55**

V   Design by the Rules **67**

VI   Iceboat Design **73**

VII   Rigs for Outracing the Wind **89**

VIII   Aerodynamics and Draft Control **109**

IX   Catamarans and Trimarans **127**

X   Real Wind and Apparent Wind **151**

XI   Hydrofoils **163**

XII   Modern Keelboats . . . and Some Speculation **171**

Suggested Reading **176**

Index **178**

Introduction

The art of stealing the power of the wind is as old as civilization itself.

Six and a half millennia ago at the very least, men of the maritime community in ancient Egypt had stretched fabric, or perhaps animal skins, within a frame, fastened the frame over a boat, then let the wind push the craft against the current, up the Nile River.

Today, men raise sails of synthetic cloth, carefully sewn and precisely battened to the shape of an airplane wing. And they go much faster and much more nearly against the direction of the wind than sailors have ever gone before.

For all but about the last century of the dozens since man began sailing, stealing the wind and stealing it more thoroughly than the next sailor was a way to power and wealth. But in the early nineteenth century, engines of iron and steel, feeding on wood and coal, began serving the purposes of navies and merchants. Within a few decades, the men for whom transport was profit or power had withdrawn their subsidies from sailing and, instead, held them out to steam. By the beginning of the twentieth century, when another engine of the new technology, this one feeding on oil, drove the first plane into the air at Kitty Hawk, sailing ships were rapidly disappearing from the seas. Huge shipyards were either being dismantled or their big stockpiles of carefully cured timber were being tossed out to make way for plates and beams of iron and steel.

But a few men still studied the wind. Some were backed by the capital of wealthy sportsmen, and others operated on limited capital of their own, but they continued to build and to sail. Though they made minor improvements, they at first stuck closely to the old designs and old ways of building. Some sought speed. Others worked on rigs that could be handled by very few men or even one man. Most wanted both. Few succeeded at first.

Gradually, though, the sailors of the twentieth century began to escape the bonds of traditional design, traditional rigging, and traditional construction. That escape is the real beginning of this book. We will discuss the ancient history of sailing and the evolution of the sailboat up to and including the clipper ship, but only for background. This book is about the accomplishments of the designers, builders, and sailors of this century.

These accomplishments are fantastic. There are sailboats in the water today, built for only a few hundred or a few thousand dollars, that could sail circles around a clipper ship if there were any left. There are water sailboats today that can go nearly twice as fast as the speed of the wind driving them. There are land yachts (sailing rigs on wheels) that can do the same thing. There are iceboats that can travel five times the speed of the wind.

Much of this has been accomplished since World War II within a growing, though widely scattered, community of designer-builders who are either outright amateurs or professionals with only small shops. Few have much capital to spend on research and testing. But still their searches go on.

One wonders how these men of the wind are accomplishing these feats without elaborate facilities for research and development. The basic ingredient is imagination, a powerful imagination that is both feeding on and fleeing from the new technology that originally drove the commercial sailing ships from the seas.

The new technology includes aerodynamics, originally a science that developed as a necessity for designing airplanes, but since then used by sailboat builders to better the designs of their sails and rigging. It includes fluid dynamics, equally useful to motor-vessel and sailboat builders in designing hull configurations to minimize resistance in passing through water. It includes modern engineering, particularly that used in designing aircraft. Twentieth century sailors have used the science of stress measurement to design boats that are both lighter and stronger by putting strength where it is needed and eliminating it where it is not needed. Finally, it includes new materials, particularly hydrocarbons, from which come synthetic sailcloth that will hold the shape that is designed into it; glues and sealers that are nearly indestructible; and plastics from which numerous parts, including hulls themselves, are built.

But even though sailors of the twentieth century are making good use of technology, they are not utterly dependent on it. Today, as planes zoom overhead at supersonic speed, it is still possible for a man to float some logs together, raise a bed sheet on a pole, and sail away for little more than the cost of some clothesline and an ax. Though a long journey over open water on such a contraption would be foolhardy, it is nonetheless possible. And, just like the most sophisticated sailboat plying the waters today, once the raft clears the shore, it is free.

Sailors of today, whether they are on such a raft or on a modern sailboat, have one thing in common. They don't need the thousands of men ashore who drill for oil and the thousands of others who refine it and haul it to the seaports. Nor do they have to make ports to deal with the sellers of gasoline, of sparkplugs, of breaker points. Sailboats of today, more than ever before, if built of good material and with reasonable care, can make long, long passages. As Sir Francis Chichester proved, they can stay at sea almost indefinitely. Such repairs as they may require can usually be accomplished aboard with little more than a few hand tools and some common sense. The wind is everywhere, just for the taking.

The wind, as power, has its shortcomings, but it is always free. Its use carries no financial or social encumbrance. And that is one of the reasons men love it.

To introduce this book and its topic properly, it remains to introduce ourselves and our reasons for writing it.

Meade Gougeon built and sailed his first boat at the age of ten. He is now a professional boat builder and a sailboat and iceboat skipper of national reputation. His firm, Gougeon Brothers Boatworks in Bay City, Michigan, is well known for its high-performance sailing craft.

Ty Knoy is a journalist and free-lance writer who sails for pleasure—like the vast majority of the sailing enthusiasts for whom we are writing. We have been friends and have sailed together for some years, and in many conversations it had become clear to us both that many casual sailors would like to know much more than they do about the design of the craft they sail and see on the water—but that the available literature was either written for the professional builder and therefore too technical and detailed for the layman, or intended for the beginning sailor and therefore concerned only with the few practical aspects of sailing theory that a sailor must know to handle a boat.

There was nothing for the sailor who had no intention of starting a boat-works, but did have an intelligent curiosity beyond the smattering of rote learning that sailing instruction generally includes. Sailing theory, like any practical science, is not just a body of rules and formulae but a dynamic and ongoing mental discipline with a social and technological history. It is fascinating even for one who never sets foot in a boat—and of course it can immensely increase the casual sailor's understanding of his pastime and his pleasure in it.

And so we decided to write a book to fill this middle ground, to enable the nonprofessional to share with the professional an understanding of how and why sailing craft have evolved. We have explained why sailboats were built as they were in the past, why they are built as they are today, why they may be built differently in the future. Since we are not telling the reader how to built a particular boat or attempting to cover the vast history of sailing, we have been able to present the evolution of design as a continuous and logical collective effort, from the first appearance of square-riggers on the Nile, through the eras of commercial sailing, the beginnings of yacht racing, and the technologically fruitful development of iceboating, to the amazingly efficient craft of today.

It is an exciting story. We hope that you will find that we have told it well.

Bay City, Michigan   MEADE GOUGEON
January 1973   TY KNOY

I Early Developments in Rigs and Hulls

Good shipwrights and good sailors, or the lack of them, have meant much to all the civilizations of history.

From the time of ancient Egypt, nations and empires have flourished as their ships and their seamen became better than those of rivals. And the same nations and empires have declined as their ships and their seamen were outdone.

Over the long run, speed was the difference between the ships of an empire on the way up, and the ships of an empire on the way down. Speed of sailboats isn't often measured by stop watches. It means very little when it is. What is meaningful is to make many passages in many different conditions of weather in less time that other boats. Sailboats, during their lifetimes, must operate one day on seas as smooth as glass, on the next on seas that are breaking over the deck; on one day in wind that won't carry cigarette ashes overboard, on the next in wind that may carry the mast overboard. For a sailboat to be fast, it must outperform other boats in all possible combinations of wind and sea, or at least enough of the combinations so that its overall performance is better.

In naval warfare, speed was the thing that allowed one fleet to maneuver another into an unfavorable position; that could put an invasion force on a foreign shore before a defense could be marshaled. But, though great naval battles and amphibious invasions have often been spectacular and are cited as turning points in history, they have more often been the symptom, rather than the cause, of change. The ships and the men who have really changed the face of the earth, who have shifted power and affluence from one empire to another, have been the thousands upon thousands of merchant ships and the millions upon millions of men who built and sailed them.

Over the centuries, merchant ships have been the vehicles that carried material and wealth to enrich their nations. And for these vessels, speed (with respect to cargo capacity) meant everything. Sailors of fast ships could outwheel and outdeal slower ones. They wouldn't do it all in a day or even a year, but in the long run, the advantage was to the swift, and to the nation whose ships were swiftest. Naval battles were often merely the results of nations trying to do by force what they were unable to do with an inferior merchant fleet.

Sails, as a means of moving ships, have been used far more by the merchant marine than by navies. For only about three hundred years, from the Spanish Armada in the sixteenth century to the Napoleonic Wars in the early nineteenth, were there naval vessels powered exclusively by sail. Before that period, oars were the primary power of warships, and they used sails only for cruising. After that period, warships were powered by machinery.

But there were trading ships that relied exclusively on sailpower probably as early as Phoenicia and certainly by the time of the Golden Age of Greece (500 to 300 B.C., more or less). On a run of a few hours, ships powered by dozens of oars were faster, and, of course, they were more maneuverable. Both of these advantages were very important to warships.

For trading ships the advantages were with sailpower. Sails were much cheaper than feeding oarsmen; sails took up no room on or below deck, leaving those areas for cargo; sails were almost always faster on a long passage because they never required any sleep.

The first application of sail to ships is generally credited to tribesmen of the Nile river valley. The credit is placed there not because we are certain that that is where it belongs, but because the oldest surviving pictures of sailboats are from that area. Archaeologists date these illustrations, which consist of carvings, paintings on pottery, etc., at about 4000 B.C.

These pictures show some ships with banks of oars, some with sails, and some with both. Details on the early illustrations are sparse, but of the sailing vessels of that time, three conclusions are fairly safe: they were square-rigged; their masts stood well forward, up near the bow; and they were controlled either by steering oars or by rudders that hung over the side.

One can only guess, but the reasoning behind these early designs may have been something like this:

Suppose a child has an old rowboat, and for some reason he has never thought of a sailing boat. And then one day someone suggests to him or it occurs to him that he should put a sail on his boat. How will he go about it?

If he is in a primitive land, he will see all around him draft animals that *pull* plows, *pull* cars, *pull* logs. Men themselves, if they happen to be moving something that has to be scooted along the ground, put a rope around the thing and *pull*.

Thus the child, knowing nothing of the physics of sailboat design, will probably think of a sail as something to *pull* his boat. Accordingly he will build his mast into the rowboat as far forward as he practically can.

On the mast itself our child will probably install two crossbars, one near the top and one near the deck level, and between these crossbars (*yards*, if we may convert to the proper term) he will stretch some fabric. The fabric will be rectangular, if for no other reason than because bolts of fabric are rectangular when they come off the loom. A rectangular sail will involve no waste.

In addition to this frugal consideration, our child will probably view his whole problem of sailing as one of building an obstruction that is perpendicular to the wind. A device of irregular shape, it would seem to him, would serve no purpose, and would only complicate the problem.

The result of our little boy's endeavor will be that his rowboat will sail along very well in a straight line with the wind. If he wants to make a course sightly to either side of the wind, he will find it necessary to drag the oar on the side to which he wishes to turn. Then the sail, because it is so far forward, will constantly tend to pull the bow over and align the whole boat back up with the wind. If the course wanted is very much away from the wind, our little boy will find it constantly necessary to push with his windward oar and pull with his lee oar to fight the tendency of the boat to realign. Such a condition in a sailboat, to always head itself downwind, is called lee helm.[1]

---

[1]The opposite of lee helm is weather helm, which is the tendency of a boat always to head up into the wind. Ideally, a boat should have neither, so that if controls are left hands off, the boat will not of its own doing change course. Some designers of sailboats today prefer a slight amount of weather helm as a safety factor, on the theory that if a helmsman is swept overboard or incapacitated, the boat will turn itself up into the wind, where it will stall, then drift backward until it falls off enough to gain power, turn up, stall, and so on and on. The idea is that the boat won't go very far. The only trouble with built-in weather helm is that it slows a boat slightly. To sail a straight course, the helmsman must steer with his rudder always slightly cocked to the lee, instead of in alignment with the water passing beneath. This causes turbulence at the rudder and, therefore, increases drag. All serious racing skippers and most other skippers today prefer balanced helm.

The arrangement our hypothetical child comes up with apparently is very similar to the arrangement of that in use on the Nile, as long as 6000 years ago. And those early ships on the Nile (the best we can estimate from the drawings is that they were 40 to 50 feet long) almost certainly also had a lot of lee helm, but it didn't matter very much there. The prevailing wind on the Nile River is from north to south—in other words, parallel to the river banks and against the current.

Most of the time the Nile sailors were able to sail up the river and drift back on the current. But if the wind happened to blow somewhat across the river, instead of parallel with it, they undoubtedly experienced the same difficulty as our little boy and had to fight the bow over with the oars. At some point, probably at 30 degrees or more on the wind, the sail became more trouble than it was worth.

About 3400 B.C., the tribes of the Nile valley and the maritime communities on the banks of the Nile were politically consolidated under the pharaoh Menes, the beginning of Egypt's old kingdom. Not long after this, Egyptian ships began wandering out the mouth of the Nile and sailing east and west along the coasts of the Mediterranean. There, on the open sea, a sailing radius of 60 degrees (30 degrees on either side of the wind) was not so good. It meant that the crews of Egyptian ships at sea spent one-sixth of their time under sail and five-sixths rowing.

All those hours at the oars may have inspired someone to come up with the first major improvement in the design of the sailing ship, *moving the sail to the center.* (Moving the sail to the center worked on the Egyptian ships because their hulls below the waterline were symmetrical and because their sail was symmetrical. The best location of the sail would not necessarily be the center if the sail plan and/or the hull were shaped irregularly.) With this simple expedient of balancing, even the crudest sail was useful in a radius of 180 degrees. The advantage was that the power of the sail could no longer turn the bow. It could do no more than push the whole boat sideways (leeway). Since the pressure from the sail was at the balance point of the hull (lengthwise balance), the pressure had no leverage on either the bow or the stern and, therefore, could not turn the ship. As we would say today, the ships had balanced helm.[2] The prob-

---

[2]A brief explanation of this concept is in order here. The relevant twentieth-century technical terms are *center of lateral resistance* (CLR), and *center of effort* (CE). The CLR is the central point of the hull's resistance to moving sideways through water. Suppose a person were trying to push a boat sideways by pushing against the side of the hull with a broom handle. If, when the person pushed, the bow went away faster than the stern, the broom handle would be touching the hull forward of the CLR. If the stern went away faster than the bow, the handle would be touching the hull aft of the CLR. When the bow and stern went away together, the broom handle would be lined up

lem of balancing helm could have been solved differently, and, in fact, it was solved differently in other cultures.

The Egyptians, before their civilization began its final decline about 1200 B.C., almost completely refined the square-rig. Many drawings of fair detail show most of the accessories in use on square-riggers of just a century ago. Among the Egyptians' inventions were braces, which were control lines from the ends of the yard to the deck to change the angle of the sail to the wind; sheets, which were lines from the lower corners of the sail to the deck, used to control the angle and, to a certain extent, the shape of the sail as well as to hold the sail against the wind; and brails, which were spaced along the foot of the sail and fastened there. The brails ran up the back of the sail, through blocks on the yard, and then down to the deck. The purpose of brails was to make it possible to reduce sail area quickly, without lowering the yard or sending anyone aloft. The sail was simply drawn up to the yard by hauling on the lines at the deck, much as one draws a venetian blind to the top of a window by pulling on cords. Brails, as they run up the back of the sail, pass through several loops sewn into the sail, so that as the sail is drawn up, it is also gathered.

The biggest weakness of Egyptian ships was probably in the construction of their hulls. Egypt has no trees fit to build a ship. The best of a bad choice of woods was acacia, a soft, coarse-grained wood, similar to willow or sycamore. Yet the first shipbuilders on the banks of the Nile were forced to use it because there was no commerce to import better timber.

The result was a peculiar method of construction. Acacia logs, which were small, weak, and highly susceptible to rot, were hewn into short, thick blocks, perhaps 12 to 18 inches thick and 10 or 15 feet long. These blocks were simply fitted and pegged together in a dish shape, somewhat the way an Eskimo would build an igloo, only elongated and upside down.

---

with the CLR. The CE refers to the sail plan (which means all the sails taken as a whole) of a ship. The central point of all the force of wind acting on this sail plan is the CE. The trick to designing a balanced helm is to place the CE directly above the CLR. If this is achieved, then the sidethrust of the sails has no leverage to turn the ship. If the CE is forward or aft of the CLR the ship will have, respectively, weather helm or lee helm (see footnote 1). Further discussion of CE and CLR would be pointless for the scope of this book, and perhaps any other book, because while they make a neat theoretical discussion, they are not so neat in reality. More on the topic can be obtained from any of a dozen or more books on yacht design, which will include details on the following complications, here offered only as food for thought: (1) the CLR shifts if a ship is loaded heavily in the stern but not in the bow, and vice-versa (and in a small boat this includes a person walking from the bow to the stern or vice-versa); (2) the CLR differs with speed because the pressure of passing water will increase on some areas of the hull, decrease on others; (3) wave action alone will cause the CLR to shift radically; (4) boats with centerboards have a different CLR for every position of the board; (5) the CE usually varies on every point of sail; (6) the CE shifts as sails are reefed or as some of the sails in a sail plan are furled.

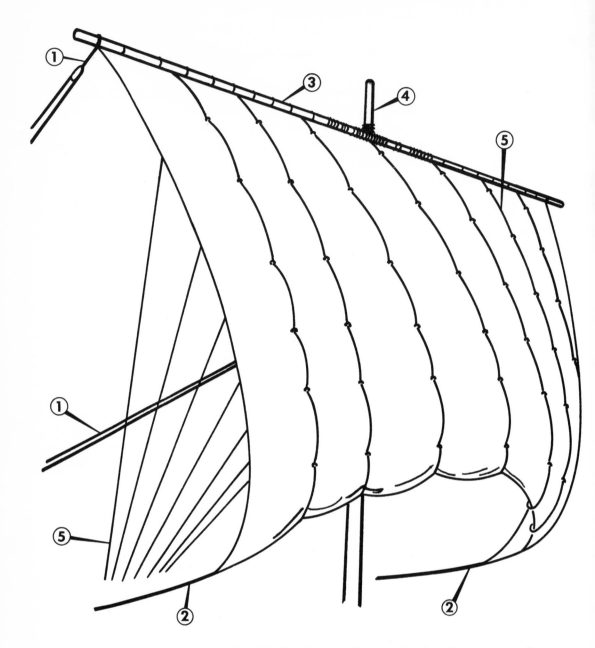

SQUARE SAIL CONTROL LINES. The basic mechanisms for handling square sails have not changed since the time of ancient Egypt. Lines run from each corner of the sail to the deck. The upper pair of lines (1) are called braces, and the lower pair (2) are called sheets. On most square rigs, whether from ancient Egypt or from the clipper ships of the nineteenth century, the yardarm (3) is permanently attached to the mast (4). Mariners of ancient Egypt, Greece, and Rome, whose ships generally had only one or two sails, used brails (5), a set of lines which ran through rings up the back of the sail, over the yardarm, and down to the deck, and the illustration shows the sail partially shortened. However, on later ships with several masts and sails, the use of brails was not possible because it would have involved a hundred or so lines. Instead, men were sent aloft to furl and unfurl the sails by hand.

But in spite of the great thickness of the hulls (they had no ribs and no keel), they were still flimsy. All pictures of any detail show a double rope "girdle" wrapped all the way around the hulls just above the waterline and another double rope wrapped around the stem and stern and running over the deck. These ropes were kept tight by twisting them together like a tourniquet. Their purpose, obviously, was to keep the pressure of the water from exploding the blocks upward and outward.

In addition to being flimsy and subject to fast deterioration, the coarse-grained wood probably soaked up a tremendous amount of water, which must have made the ships incredibly heavy and unwieldy.

Even so, the Egyptians marshaled enough of these crafts to bring Phoenicia, an emerging civilization more or less in present-day Lebanon, under its control by 2900 B.C. With this conquest came access to cedar trees.

Cedar is a fine ship timber. It is strong, its grain is tight, and its own natural oil seals it against water and greatly retards deterioration. The logs are of such size that beams and planks can be hewn to 75 feet or more in length. The Egyptians towed much of this timber back to the Nile and turned it over to their shipwrights.

But it didn't do them as much good as it could have. The shipbuilding community, already thirty to fifty generations old at the time, couldn't break the habit of building ships out of blocks. For the most part, it seems, they took the fine cedar logs, cut them into small pieces, and went on building the way they always had. The results were weak, heavy-going ships that, if they held together, lasted a lot longer.

The Egyptians were the first and last to build ships of blocks. Beginning with the vessels of Phoenicia and Greece, the two powers that vied for control of the Mediterranean as Egypt declined, ships were built of planking, eventually over ribs and strong keels. Planked hulls in the Mediterranean and in China have always been carvel-built (the planks butted edge to edge), while in the area of the Baltic, the Northmen and Germans always built lapstrake hulls (the planks overlapping with the edges riveted together).

It apparently never occurred to the Egyptians to put more than one sail on a ship, but merchant ships of the Romans, who were taking control of the Mediterranean from Greece during the time of Christ, commonly had three sails: a big, square mainsail; a triangular topsail; and an artemon.

The three corners of the topsail were secured to either end of the main yard and to the masthead, which extended above the yard. This topsail was small and merely an extension of the main. It was also the first of many extensions of the effort to get more and more canvas perpendicular to the wind.

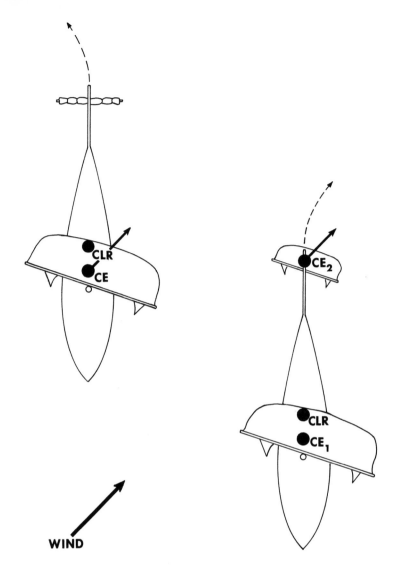

WIND

AN ANCIENT STEERING SAIL. Before the time of Christ, sailors in the Mediterranean were using the artemon (the small sail in the illustration) to aid in steering. The two illustrations show the same vessel with the artemon furled and unfurled. The dot marked CLR (center of lateral resistance) in both illustrations is the axis on which the hull turns. The CE (center of effort) in both illustrations is the center of force exerted by the sail. In the illustration on the left there is only one CE, and since it is behind the CLR, the stern of the vessel will be forced to the right, which will cause the bow to head to the left (dotted line). In the other illustration there are two CEs. CE_2 (in the artemon) has much longer leverage on the CLR than CE_1, and so forces the bow of the ship to the right. Seamen of ancient times used this method (in addition to rudders) to steer. Their artemons, like their mainsails, were fitted with braces, sheets, and brails (see previous illustration), allowing them to control the artemon from the deck. To keep a straight course they sailed with the artemon half furled. The artemon was simply a miniature square sail. Its yardarm was attached to a mast which ran out over the bow at about a 45-degree angle upward.

The third sail on Roman ships was something genuinely new. Though they probably didn't invent it themselves, the Romans may have been the first to use it extensively. It was the artemon, a square sail perhaps a fourth the size of the main. The yard was at the end of a spar that protruded upward and out in front of the bow. The sail was controlled by braces, sheets, and brails, the ends of which all ran aft to the deck. Its purposes may have been partly for power, but mostly it was an aid to steering.

By manipulating the artemon with the control lines, the Roman sailors could deliberately unbalance the helm of their ships, causing them to turn. If you assume that a Roman ship had balanced helm when under main and topsails alone, then unfurling the artemon would, of course, move the center of effort forward and create lee helm. If you assume balanced helm under main and topsails with the artemon half-furled, then unfurling the artemon would create lee helm while furling it completely would create weather helm. Thus the artemon could be used to turn the ship in either direction. Whether such was the case or not, it is theoretically possible.

The Roman ships were big, up to 175 feet long. They were apparently nearly a third of that in breadth and slow to turn by the rudders, especially since the rudders were mounted on the sides a quarter of the way forward from the stern. With the artemon the ship's heading could be changed even when there was little or no way on, such as when maneuvering in port. A rudder is, of course, worthless unless water is moving by the hull.

The Roman square-riggers, like the Egyptian square-riggers, could sail comfortably as long as the wind was abeam or farther aft. How high up into the wind the Roman vessels could sail is anybody's guess. On big ships, such as the ones that hauled grain from Alexandria to Rome, windward ability couldn't have mattered much. Captains on passages of that length could choose their routes to keep the wind astern.

For smaller vessels, such as coastal freighters and fishing boats, the problem was different. Operating in a small area with round trips in a shorter period of time, the crews had to take the wind as it came. Sailing to windward was important. The first invention in the Mediterranean to meet the need was the fore-and-aft spritsail, apparently used as the mainsail on smaller vessels by both the Greeks and the Romans.

A boat rigged for a fore-and-aft spritsail has a single mast that stands vertically very near the bow. The sail is rectangular, and one of its sides is fastened all along the mast so that the sail swings about the mast, back and forth over the deck, like a gate swings on a post. Supporting the free side of the sail is a boom, hinged to the mast at deck level and running diagonally upward to the top corner of the free side of the sail.

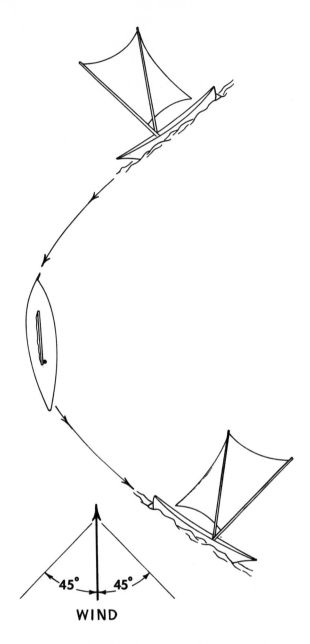

45°   **45°**

WIND

FORE-AND-AFT SPRITSAIL. This rig appeared in the Mediterranean at about the time of Christ. The sail and the diagonal boom, or sprit, swing freely behind the mast like a wind vane. With this rig, a boat can make headway against the wind. The sail develops power up to about 45 degrees of the wind by sailing a zigzag course. The illustration shows the boat going through one of the zigs. In the center position, the sail is developing no power and the boat must coast until it gets off on the other course where the sail can fill again. The rig was used for fishing and coastal transport, which require many more maneuvers than long hauls. Notice that during the turn, the crew had to take the lower, aft corner of the sail and pass it over the boom. Otherwise the sail would lie against the boom. The rig was used only on small boats. In large sizes the boom would have been too heavy to manage.

The angle of the sail was controlled by two lines, one running from the top of the boom, the other running from the lower free corner of the sail. As the boat went from one tack to the other, the free corner at the bottom of the sail was passed over the boom, so that the sail always billowed away from the boom, never against it.

The rig probably worked well to windward. The mast provided a solid, unfluttering edge to cut the wind. In addition, the rig was no impediment in maneuvering the bow of the boat through the wind (called tacking or coming about). During the turn, the sail just swung along behind the mast like a wind vane. In making a course upwind, a boat rigged with a fore-and-aft spritsail just zigzags, the same way a sloop does today.

No such maneuver is possible in a square-rigger. Square-riggers can zigzag upwind, but when changing from one tack to the other, they must turn in the other direction and bring the stern, not the bow, through the wind. This maneuver, loosely called jibing,[3] involves a turn of about 270 degrees, half of it opposite the desired direction of travel, and is expensive in both time and distance.

Two men could easily handle a good-sized boat rigged with a fore-and-aft spritsail. The problems with the rig were that it was difficult if not impossible to reef, and that it was very unhandy to hoist and lower.

Some sketchy carvings from classical times survive today that show the fore-and-aft spritsail on the bow of a large vessel that has a square-rigged mainsail. Its purpose in this tandem was undoubtedly the same as the artemon. Another interesting drawing from the same period shows *two* fore-and-aft spritsails winged out on either side of the *same mast*. We presume the boat would be running before the wind or on a broad reach and that one of the sails was lowered for sailing close to the wind.

During the Middle Ages another type of fore-and-aft sail appeared in the Mediterranean. The rig had a mast near the center of the boat, and on this mast was hoisted a long, thin yard. All along the yard was fastened one side of a triangular sail. Control lines were attached to the free corner of the triangle and to the pole. The setup is called a lateen rig. A slightly modified version of it survives today on the popular Alcort *Sailfish* and *Sunfish*. The Alcort sails differ in that they have a boom along the lower side of the triangle in addition to the yard on the upper side.

---

[3]Jibing does not actually mean this whole maneuver, but only that part of it where the stern goes through the wind. The moment is completely uneventful on a square-rigger, but on boats with fore-and-aft rigs the sail slams over as the wind catches its back side. Crews must be careful to sheet their sail home as far as possible as the moment arrives for the jibe. The sheets then restrict the slamming to a short arc, which is easier on rigging and nerves.

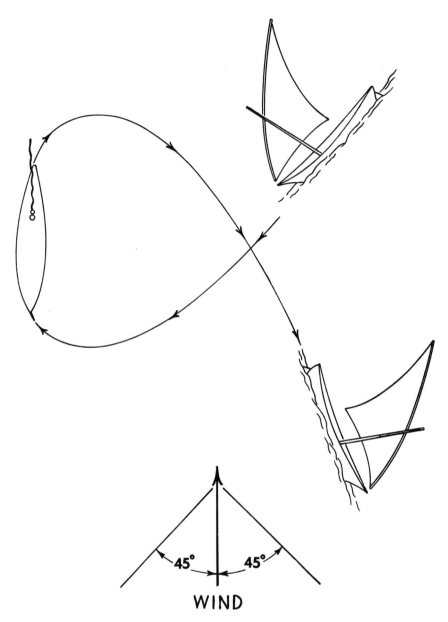

WIND

THE LATEEN SAIL. This rig appeared on small boats in the Mediterranean during the Middle Ages. The triangular sail is supported along the top by a long yardarm. Like the fore-and-aft spritsail (see previous illustration), a boat with this rig works up to within about 45 degrees of the wind, permitting the boat to sail to weather. However, it must turn away from the wind, not through it, so that the crew can wrestle the yardarm and sail over to the other side of the mast. If the boat turned through the wind, the sail would be blowing against the mast when the boat got over to the other tack. Except for this problem, the sail is probably superior to the fore-and-aft spritsail. A sail similar to this was used by ancient South Sea Islanders on double canoes. Arab mariners also used this sail, probably before Europeans, but they put the yard and the sail between the two legs of an A-frame mast. A boat rigged in that fashion is called a dhow (pronounced "dow").

Precisely the same rig as is used on the Alcorts of today was used by the sea people of the South Pacific Ocean who migrated off the Asian mainland, beginning during the classical times of the Mediterranean, and, over the next thousand years, island-hopping eastward in big double canoes, reaching the Hawaiian Islands (and, according to some theorists, the West Coast of South America) about 700 A.D. Though anthropologists have them divided into several subraces, the people today are commonly called Polynesians.

Polynesian canoes were fitted with two or three lateen sails which, like today's Alcorts, had both yard and boom. However, the Polynesian sails were extremely long and not very high. The yard and the boom were, of course, fastened to each other, but at their open ends they also were bowed abruptly toward each other, though they did not touch. Within these bows a deep, circular notch was cut into the sail material. This strange configuration has spawned the term "claw sail" for the Polynesian version of the rig, probably because the shape of the sail reminds one of a lobster's claw. The variation was apparently only for decorative purposes. We can discern no aerodynamic or other practical advantages.

While the Polynesians were in the midst of their migration across the South Pacific, marauding barbarians were leading a migration out of northern Europe and western Asia and pushing back the frontiers of the Roman Empire.

The Western Roman Empire disintegrated in the fifth century A.D., and with it went law, order, and, therefore, commerce. In a few years, all western Europe became a wilderness dotted with self-sufficient little fiefdoms between which robbers and savage nomads roamed at will, bothered only by each other.

The Mediterranean, no longer patrolled by the Roman navy, soon filled with pirates and Arab raiders. Such commerce as there was moved in small vessels that were lightly loaded and that darted from port to port under lateen sails, eluding pirates either with speed or by sailing high into the wind. Even so, traders in those days seldom ventured far from familiar shores.

The migration down through Europe to the Mediterranean was nothing new even during the Middle Ages. The Roman legions had held back the tide—or rather had allowed it only to seep in—but the migration predated Rome and, in fact, scholars writing as far back as ancient Egypt complained of it.

What eventually happened was that the barbarians settled, fraternized with those they conquered, and then themselves built new civilizations, just as had happened with the Romans and, before them, the Greeks, all of whom were at one time barbarians out of the north.

When Europe began coming out of the Middle Ages, a new era of ship-building began to unfold. After the fall of Rome, an Arab empire became solidly entrenched around the east end of the Mediterranean. The emerging European nations, and especially those with coastlines on the Atlantic, began launching voyages of exploration with the hope of circumnavigating the Arab middlemen who held control of the only known route to the rich trade with India and China. One such voyage was that of Christopher Columbus, a Genoese sailing for Spain, in the fall of 1492. The expedition unexpectedly ran into an unknown continent, with the result that Columbus was credited (falsely) with discovering the New World.

Among the migrants working down through Europe during the Middle Ages were the Northmen, a people from what is now Scandinavia. The first of them were raiders, called Vikings, who traveled in long, open boats as they plundered coastal villages in Europe and England. Later they came as traders, conquerors, colonists, and immigrants. They also sailed to and colonized Iceland and Greenland and one of their expeditions spent a winter, about 1000 A.D. on the East Coast of North America, probably in the area of the Gulf of St. Lawrence.

The Northmen had a long tradition of seamanship and many of their descendants settled into the maritime communities of the nations of Europe that emerged from the Middle Ages. Many of the shipwrights and sailors for the voyages of exploration were big men with blond hair and blue eyes.

Just what influence these Scandinavians had on ship design in Europe isn't certain. But ships that sailed better did begin to appear during the Renaissance, as explorers were taking to the high seas.

The difference was mainly in the hulls. Instead of the round bottom, there came the concave bottom, where the sides rounded under below the waterline, but then turned down again to the keel, which ran deep in the water. The keel, too, instead of curving slowly from the stem, down through the water, and up to the stern, was long and flat. It ran deep for most of the length of the ship and then either turned up sharply to form the bow and the stern, or it connected to near-vertical end posts that formed the bow and the stern.

The results were hulls that cut through the water like a knife sliding on its sharp edge. Because of their greater length under water (with respect to overall length), they were faster. (It is axiomatic that any given hull configuration—except the planing hull, which is a twentieth-century invention—is faster as its length is increased. But the *length at the waterline* is the factor. A hull designed so that its length at the water is nearly equal to its overall length will probably be speedier than a hull of similar length that has a shorter length at the water.) They also had a much greater amount of lateral resistance, which enabled them to sail closer to the wind. They were also easier to keep on course, but slower to turn (which is why they were easier to keep on course).

The concave hulls probably evolved from the designs of the Northmen. There was nothing remarkable about the Northmen's sails (their boats were all single-masted square-riggers), but their hulls were long and the bottoms were flat, lengthwise. Crosswise, the later Northmen boats were a shallow V with the keel protruding a few inches below the planking. These boats sailed well and it is logical that they were the antecedent of the concave design.

But even though the concave hulls were much faster and sailed much better than round bottoms, the design never did revolutionize shipbuilding. The trouble was that the design afforded far less capacity for cargo (or, in the case of warships, guns and powder) than a fat, round bottom of comparable dimension. The problem led to many compromise designs that were somewhat in between sleek sailers and fat cargo carriers.

The very same problem persists to this day for the weekend yachtsman who goes out to buy. He wants a boat that performs well and that has spacious accommodations. But sooner or later, within any given length (or any given amount of money, which is more or less in the same proportion), he will have to make up his mind how much comfort he is willing to give up for performance, or vice-versa. He can't really have it both ways.

The first ships known to have concave bottoms were the cog, a German trading vessel with a single mast and square sail, and the caravel, a Portuguese vessel of exploration that was sometimes square-rigged, sometimes rigged with two or three lateen sails. Both vessels are of the fourteenth and fifteenth centuries. Both had rudders mounted over the stern instead of over the side, which was something new in Europe, though the junks of China had had stern rudders for centuries.

The caravel made up most of the fleet of Portuguese explorers at the time of Prince Henry the Navigator (1394–1460), the famous patron of expeditions down the west coast of Africa. Ships of those expeditions were invariably rigged with lateen sails because the prevailing winds along the coast are out of the north and the ships had to beat their way home on the return passage.

Of Columbus' three ships, the *Nina* and the *Pinta* were apparently caravels or something of that type. They were, of course, Spanish ships, not Portuguese.

When Columbus sailed from Palos the *Nina* had lateen sails, but on the way out the expedition put into the Canary Islands and Columbus had the

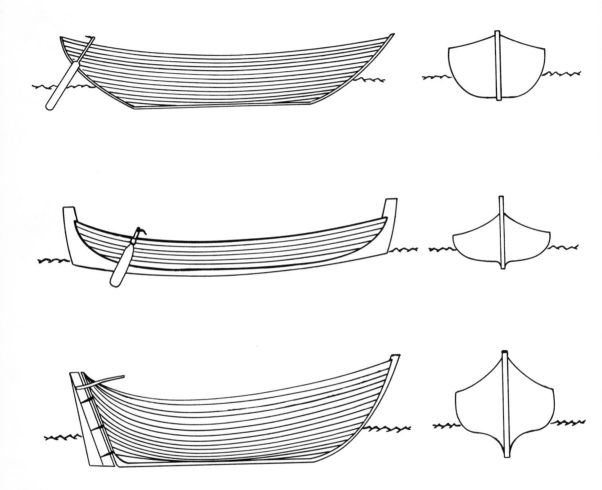

EVOLUTION OF HULL SHAPES. Though we cannot tell for certain from the illustrations that survive, it is believed that hulls of ancient times and in the Middle Ages had bottoms that were rounded, as in the top illustration here. Such hulls could not have worked very well to weather because there is not much of a plane to prevent leeway. The long boats of the Northmen (center) were an improvement because the keel protruded below the planking, providing a greater plane of resistance. The plane also was extended beyond the ends of the planking, which further increased resistance. Immigration of Northmen shipwrights into Europe probably brought about the concave bottom (bottom illustration), in which the planking of ships is rounded under, but turns down again to a deep-running keel. Hansa Cogs were apparently the first hulls of this general type. The hulls of Portuguese exploration ships were also of this configuration.

Nina converted to a square-rigger. She was apparently having trouble keeping up with the fleet, and since the voyage was to be east and west, there was to be little need for sailing to windward.

One accessory to the square sail that did help it work to windward was apparently the invention of the Northmen. It was bowlines, which were standard equipment on square sails from the time of the explorations on. Bowlines were pieces of cord, one end of which were sewn at intervals into the side edges of the sail. These pieces of cord, usually three, came together at their other ends and joined into a line that ran forward to some bitt or cleat. There it was pulled tight when the ship was going to weather. The result was that the leading edge of the sail was stiffened and fluttered less as it cut into the wind. Bowlines were sewn into both leeches and used according to which tack the ship was on.

Very early in the age of exploration the patterns of prevailing winds on all the oceans were charted, and ever after until the end of commercial sailing, the basic rigging of sea-going vessels was square. Square sails work well in following winds, and in transoceanic passages, captains simply followed courses that would keep the wind at their sterns.

Over the years, ships were fitted with more and more sails until they stood six high on three different masts, as in the case of the clippers (about 1850). Mixed in with the square sails were staysails along with a fore-and-aft sail (at first a lateen sail, later a gaff-rig sail) on the aftermost mast. The staysails were for extra power and the fore-and-aft sail was to aid steering and to balance the helm, but the main fare was square sails. One colossus, built in 1903 during the death struggle of sailing ships, had five masts, each with six square sails. She was the *Preussen,* a German vessel that was over 400 feet long and carried 50,000 square feet of canvas. Like many of the very last sailing ships, the *Preussen* was built of iron and steel. Her masts and yards were steel tubing, and her lines, many hauled by steam winches, were wire, cable, or chain rather than hemp.

The concave hull, as it turned out, was the final refinement in hulls during the commercial sailing era. Explorers who sailed in the South Pacific did notice that the islanders' double sailing canoes could run circles around their own craft, but no multihull vessel was ever built in the West to enter commercial service, except some very recent ones put on tourist excursion runs.

Some of the islanders steered their double canoes under sail without rudders or steering oars. The technique was to put long, thin boards straight down into the water to serve as fins for lateral resistance. Since the canoes operated a great deal of the time off of beaches, the boards were only put down after the craft was under way, and then they were only lashed to the frame or the hulls. The islanders apparently steered

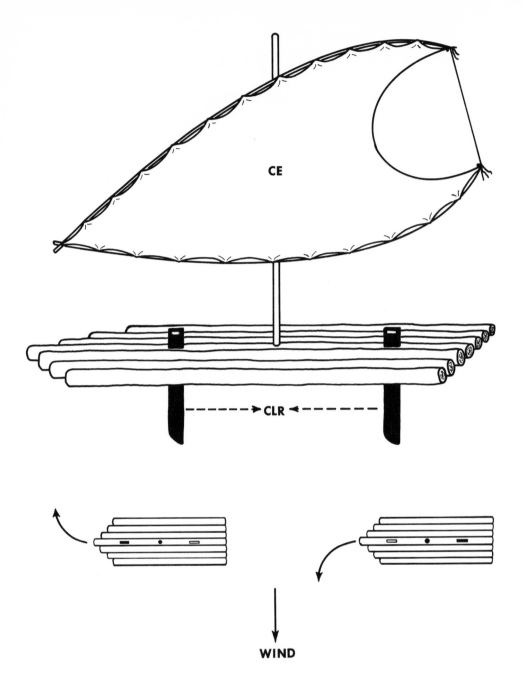

CE

CLR

WIND

STEERING WITHOUT A RUDDER. *Prehistoric men on the West Coast of South America sailed balsa rafts and steered them not with a rudder, but by moving the center of lateral resistance. The top drawing is such a raft with two finlike boards. Each board can be raised and lowered. When both boards are down, their combined CLR is directly beneath the center of effort of the sail. The raft sails straight ahead. If the forward board only is pulled up, the raft turns to lee, as in the lower right drawing. If the after board only is pulled up, the raft heads to weather, as in the lower left drawing. The same system was used by some South Sea Islanders to control double canoes in their migrations across the Pacific.*

their craft by simply moving the boards around, balancing and unbalancing the helm to sail a straight course or to turn.

European explorers operating in the East also ran into Chinese merchant ships that were trading, as they had done for centuries, down into the Philippines and along the coasts of Southeast Asia. The Chinese ships were extremely large, with several decks cut up into hundreds of compartments. Hundreds of merchants sailed on a single ship, each using a compartment as his own private office and warehouse.

The ships, which Westerners all lump under the term "junk," had several interesting features, among them the stern rudder. It is possible that word of the design seeped through Arabia and into Europe during the Middle Ages and influenced the gradual change in European ships to stern rudders, rather than the rudder-over-the-side design, which had been the rule since the beginning of time.

The junks carried sails that were something new to Europeans. The fabric was slatted with thin pieces of wood that ran the entire width of the cloth and were spaced two or three feet apart all the way up. The sails, which were four-sided, were fastened to the mast by the slats with about a fourth of the sail area in front of the mast, the rest behind. The arrangement, called lug sail, was for counterbalance, and the sail could be hauled in effortlessly, even in a stiff wind. The masts had running stays from the top only so that the slats could slide freely up and down.

Lines, running from the leech end of the slats to the deck, enabled the crew to control the shape of the sail, slat by slat. The sail was very efficient and easy to handle even in very large sizes, and the Chinese seamen were expert with it. The rig would have worked well to windward, specially on the tack where the mast was on the weather side of the sail. But the hull of the junk had little lateral resistance, and the Chinese seemed to care little about sailing to windward anyway. Their voyages to the Philippines were carefully timed each year so they could run before the monsoons on the return voyage.

Reefing was simply a matter of partially dropping the halyard and securing slats and cloth as they fell onto each other at the foot of the sail. All of this could be accomplished in a few seconds without sending anyone aloft. The system is still one of the best ever devised.

The ideas of the Chinese rig were never seriously assimiliated by Westerners during commercial sailing, though yachtsmen in the twentieth century are making some use of them. One wonders if a clipper hull, had it been fitted with junk-type sails, could have been even faster. It almost certainly could have been manned by about a third of the crew required for the Western-type rig.

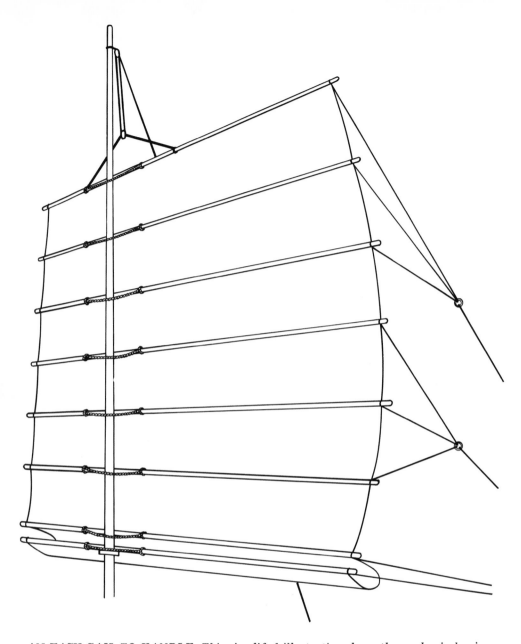

AN EASY SAIL TO HANDLE. This simplified illustration shows the mechanical principles of the slatted lug sail, common thousands of years ago in the Far East. It is most commonly associated with what Westerners call junks. If a sudden storm makes it necessary, the sail can be shortened very quickly simply by lowering the halyard. The slats, in between the panels of fabric, fall on top of each other at the bottom, where the slats are lashed in a bunch by ties (not shown). In this illustration, the sail has been partially shortened and the second slat is almost touching the first. It is possible to shorten the sail any number of slats because the control lines are fastened by "crow-feet" bridles to each slat. Aside from being handier, this system is much better than brails because the reduced sail ends up at the bottom of the mast, not the top. Notice also that part of the sail is in front of the mast. This arrangement counterbalances the force on the sail and makes the sail controllable with only slight tugs on the lines.

There was a lug sail in Europe, though, long before the West had contact with China. It appeared on fishing boats operating out of ports on the Brittany coast in the Middle Ages. The sail, however, was not slatted. It hung from a single yard and had rows of reefing ties. One might describe it as a four-sided version of the lateen sail, and the yard could be wrestled around so that it always was on the lee side of the mast, as was done with the European version of the lateen sail. During the Napoleonic Wars, the French navy had dispatch and coastal patrol boats rigged with lug sails. The boats had as many as three masts, each of which carried a lug sail and lug topsail.

The staysail, which commonly came to fly over the bowsprit of big ships of the West, was apparently an invention of the Dutch. The sail is cut more or less as a right triangle and the long side is secured all along a forward-going stay. The jib in the sloop rigs of today is an example of it. Of all the sails from the commercial era of sailing, it is by far the most common on sailing machines of the twentieth century.

The Dutch, who had only small craft for a navy during their revolt against Spanish rule in the late 1500's, commonly used a forestay sail in combination with fore-and-aft spritsail during the revolution.

Two or three generations later, if that long, the Dutch came up with the gaff rig, a design that is still common on larger yachts today and was the antecedent of the Marconi rig.

The gaff-rig sail is four-sided with the forward side fastened all along the mast, just like the fore-and-aft spritsail. But instead of the sail being supported by a boom from the mast at deck level to the upper, after corner, the upper edge of the canvas was fastened all along a yard (the gaff). One end of this gaff was hinged to the mast and slid up and down it. The gaff was raised and lowered by halyards and its free end supported by tackle running to the masthead, which, of course, had to be higher than the gaff. Later on the Dutch got around to adding a boom, hinged to the mast at one end, to which the lower edge of the sail was fastened.

The rig is similar to the French lug sail except that no part of it is forward of the mast. In fact, the leading edge is fastened along the mast.

The gaff rig is very convenient, especially when sailing in constricted waters, such as canals, which the Dutch did a lot of. The crew of a gaff-rigger can change tack simply by steering the bow through the wind. They do not even need to uncleat the sheets.

The same is true of the Marconi, which is practically the universal main-stay on small sailboats today. Because it has only one halyard, the Marconi rig is even more convenient than the gaff rig. But the Marconi rig was not a development of commercial sailing. It was the invention of the twentieth century.

II Less Weight and More Speed

Little progress in speed under sail was made in the two centuries following Columbus' voyage to America. Many contend that the art even slid backward in those years, roughly 1500 to 1700.

To be fair, though, one must realize that speed was not the first concern of builders and mariners. Columbus' voyage was at the beginning of an era in which ships were venturing on vast oceans. Destinations were only vaguely known and weather along the routes was often fierce, always unpredictable.

If one keeps these things in mind and also realizes that a voyage to "the New World" took sixty or seventy days, probably ten times the average length of voyages between port calls around Europe, one can forgive the ugly, tublike vessels. Ships probing the New World needed a huge capacity for provisions, and they needed heavy timbers in their frames to withstand the seas.

In short, the overriding concern during the explorations was just getting there and getting back, and speed was given little thought. An analogy is with the space voyages of today. For all of today's thousands of people working on the space program, just making the journey is the thing. No one is complaining—yet—that a trip to the moon takes three or four days each way.

The beginnings of colonization made voyages to the New World more common, but still there was no great improvement in speed. Nor, apparently, was there much improvement in navigation: 128 years after Columbus, the beloved *Mayflower* inadvertently established the colony of Massachusetts when she took sixty-six days to cross the Atlantic and miss her mark by over 500 miles (she had set sail from Southampton for Virginia, but ended up in Cape Cod Bay).

But eventually a situation arose that put a premium on pure speed. The time was roughly 225 years after Columbus, the place was the English colonies on the eastern coast of North America, and the situation was a trade restriction imposed by the English on their colonies. In a policy designed to improve the financial position of the mother country, the English limited the amount of trade with countries other than England the colonists could engage in.

The result, of course, was smuggling. As happens with trade restrictions, prices of contraband goods were driven so high that profits were high enough to cover high risks. The only problem was getting the contraband past the Royal Navy a reasonable amount of the time. Since it was impractical for a smuggler to arm his ship and shoot it out, the answer to the problem was speed. Thus in the early 1700's, in clandestine shipyards, in makeshift ports and anchorages all the way from Massachusetts to Georgia, the Americans began to earn the reputation they enjoy to this day of being the builders and sailors of the fastest sailing machines in the world.

Colonial smugglers were able to take advantage of several unhappy features of English warships, among them square rigging, which has little ability to go to windward; high freeboard and high structures above deck, both of which caused windage and further cut down ability to windward; extremely heavy construction, which increased weight; heavy armament (up to three gun decks, each with a score or more of cannon), which again increased weight; and heavy ballasting, tons upon tons of rocks and/or pig iron in the bilge, necessary to counterbalance the top-heaviness caused by the first four features, but further increasing all-up weight.

It would be charitable to describe these ships as slow and lumbering. Yet they suited the unimaginative naval tactics of the time—two lines of these floating forts would simply drift up to each other and blast away.

Such craft, however, were ill-suited for pursuit of the ships that were developed by the colonists.

The economics of smuggling worked on the side of the colonists. Since the margin of profit on cargo was so high, it was not necessary for smuggling ships to carry big loads to have a lucrative run. This important fact had two effects: smuggling ships were much lighter than Royal Navy ships of comparable dimensions; and the hulls of the smuggling ships could be designed for speed with little regard for capacity of the hold. In other words, the hulls could be long and thin, with great deadrise (V-like bottom) and long, sharp bows and sterns.

Of course, long, sharp hulls were nothing new when the colonists began building ships—hulls of the cogs and caravels were long and sharp. But the configuration had been forgotten for several hundred years. The colonists revived the design and eventually carried it to a greater extreme.

Another economic fact of smuggling worked in favor of speed: Smuggling ships were subject to a high rate of loss, and therefore they were cheaply built. And being cheaply built, they were of light construction, with the result that all-up weight was less than it would have been with the English standard of construction.

But the crowning feature, which practically became standard on all medium-size American ships and has been standard on American yachts for decades, was that the schooners were, for the most part, fore-and-aft rigged. Most were schooners; some were sloops.

A sloop in colonial America was the same thing as a sloop today. It is a craft with a fore-and-aft rig on a single mast. (In the days of the smugglers though, the sails were gaff-rigged.)

The schooner, according to American tradition, was invented at Gloucester, Massachusetts, in 1713. This may or may not be true, depending on how you define a schooner. Today, a vessel is designated a schooner only on the basis of its rig, and the rig was not invented in 1713. It was in use in Holland at least a century earlier. Today's definition, which we will use in this book, is a vessel with at least two masts, the forward mast being the same height or shorter than the other mast(s), *and* all masts being rigged with fore-and-aft sails. There are many variations within this definition.

Most schooners of the colonial period and of the early years of the Republic were two- or three-masted. In addition to the fore-and-aft sails, most of the early schooners also carried a small, square-rig topsail above the gaff on the main mast, and sometimes on the foremast also. These topsails were used for running (with the wind), but not for beating (against the wind). It is an important point that these topsails, yardarms and all, were on halyards and were lowered to the deck and stowed when the schooner was beating. The yardarms of square-rigged ships were permanently fastened to the masts and were not set up to be lowered.

Why is it important that the topsail yardarms of schooners could be lowered? It has to do with weight distribution.

We have already established that square-riggers tended to be heavier than fore-and-aft riggers, and it should need no explaining that it takes more power—more wind or more sails or both—to move a heavy ship at a given speed than it does to move a lighter one. But of as much importance as the amount of weight is the consideration of where the weight is located.

Any object has a center of gravity (CG), and for ships, it is best that the center be somewhere near the waterline. In fact, the lower the CG is, the less likely the ship is to get knocked down or to turn turtle.

Assume for a moment that there is a vessel that has a CG right at the waterline. That CG can be lowered (with respect to the hull) by adding weight (ballast) below the waterline. The CG of that same vessel will be raised by adding weight above the waterline.

If the CG is very much above the waterline, the vessel would be almost as likely to sail upside down as right side up.

Of course if one must add, say, 100 pounds on deck, which is 10 feet above the waterline, this can be counterbalanced by putting another 100 pounds in the bilge, if the bilge is 10 feet below the waterline. Then the ship will be as stable as it ever was, but it will be a total of 200 pounds heavier.

But here is the hooker. Suppose one puts a weight (a yardarm, for instance) up on the mast 100 feet above the waterline and that yardarm weighs 100 pounds. Now to counterbalance the weight of that yard, one cannot put just 100 pounds in the bilge 10 feet below waterline; one must put in 1,000 pounds. The reason is that the yardarm, while weighing only one-tenth of what the ballast does, has ten times the leverage of the ballast.

The result is that the all-up weight is increased 1,100 pounds to accommodate a simple yardarm. If one multiplies this by the dozens of yardarms, rigging hardware (iron in those days), etc., one can understand why square-riggers were such heavy beasts.

Sweden, while preparing for her invasion of Germany during the Thirty Years' War, had a sad experience with a warship that was built and fitted without enough regard for weight distribution.

In August 1628, amid cheers of thousands gathered at the quay of the Royal Palace, a 180-foot galleon sailed out into Stockholm's harbor on a Sunday afternoon.

The ship was the *Vasa*. She was on her maiden voyage with dozens of wives and children of her officers aboard for a parade cruise around the

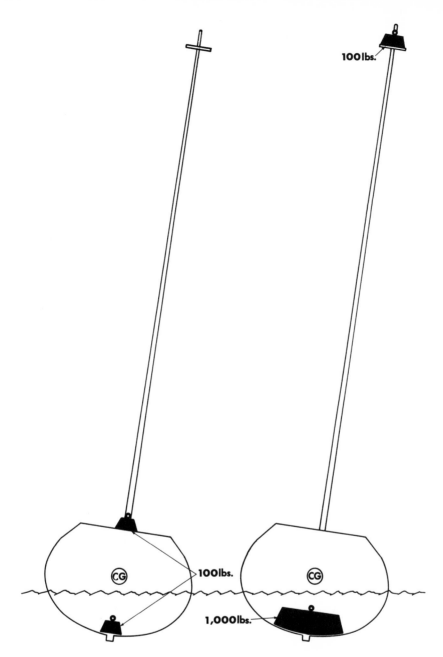

WEIGHT ALOFT REDUCES SPEED. Weight aloft indirectly cuts heavily into a boat's potential for speed, because weight aloft must have heavy ballast for counterbalance. In the cutaway end view at left, a deck weight of 100 pounds is counterbalanced by a mere 100 pounds of ballast because the weights are an equal distance from the vessel's center of gravity. In the drawing at right, the 100 pounds that was on deck has been moved high up into the rigging. Now a much heavier ballast weight is required as a counterbalance. If the 100 pounds is ten times as far from the center of gravity as the ballast, then ten times as much ballast, or 1,000 pounds, will be required because the weight aloft has ten times the leverage of the weight below. The 100 pounds on deck forces the ship designer to increase the all-up weight only 200 pounds, but the 100 pounds aloft forces an increase of 1,100 pounds. The added displacement and wetted surface slows the ship.

harbor. Less than a mile from her berth, while sailors high in the rigging were still breaking out sails, *Vasa* rolled to port and did not recover. Cheers along the harbor changed to gasps of horror as sailors aboard waited breathlessly for the next wave. When it came, it heeled *Vasa* even farther. Solid water began cascading through gunports. In a few minutes she filled and her ballast, which was not heavy enough to keep her upright, was nonetheless heavy enough to take her to the bottom in 110 feet of water off Beckholmen. Some fifty lives were lost before rescue boats could get out. *Vasa's* bulk was raised (1959-61) and is now a permanent museum at Djurgarden, on the harbor.

Not many ships have been out of balance so badly as to suffer the fate of *Vasa*, but there are records of plenty that were balanced poorly enough so that their rigs had to be reduced from what was originally put on them.

Fore-and-aft rigging involves less weight aloft on any given size vessel than does square-rigging. On colonial sloops and schooners there were long, heavy gaffs aloft, but that was about all except for the masts themselves. Over the years the gaffs gradually became shorter and shorter. Today, the gaff-rig has all but been eliminated by the wide popularity of the Marconi sail, an invention of the twentieth century.

After the American Revolution, schooners became increasingly popular as legitimate commercial vessels, particularly as coasters, fishing boats, pilot boats, and Great Lakes boats. Fore-and-aft riggers, being more weatherly, are much more manageable in constricted waters, and they were labor savers. It takes only half a dozen men to sail a large schooner, whereas it takes four or five times that many to run a square-rigger. Fore-and-afters are run almost entirely from the deck. Square-riggers have to have dozens of men ready to scurry up into the rigging to trim sails every time the ship changes course or to furl or unfurl sail if the wind velocity changes.

The only trouble with fore-and-afters from a commercial sailing point of view is that they cannot be scaled up indefinitely. The sails become impractically large on masts of about 100 feet or over. There have indeed been some very large boats rigged fore-and-aft. Masts of the America's Cup boats before World War II, for instance, were considerably more than 100 feet, and all were fore-and-aft-rigged, but these boats were backed by hundreds of thousands of dollars, a good part of it spent on maintaining crews that could handle such acreages of sail, and another good part of it spent on designing, building, and maintaining spars and standing rigging that could withstand the pressures. Even so, those monstrosities had to hightail it into port if the wind got anywhere above a fair breeze. They could not sail under all conditions of wind and sea without great risk of having their rigging either damaged or demolished.

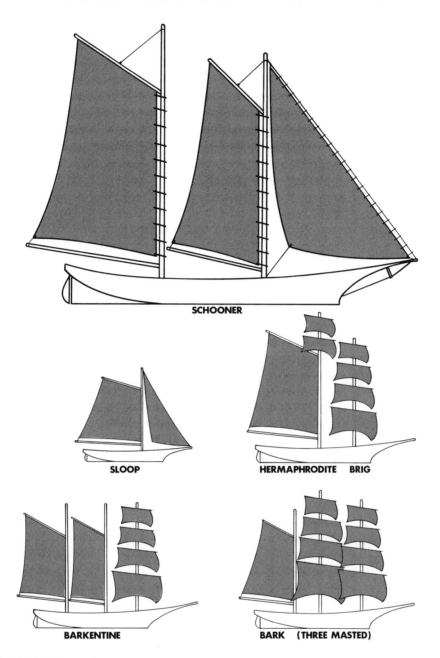

SCHOONER

SLOOP

HERMAPHRODITE BRIG

BARKENTINE

BARK (THREE MASTED)

GAFF-RIG APPLICATIONS. The invention of gaff rigging, apparently in the Nether-
lands in the 1500's, made it practical to fore-and-aft-rig large ships. The use of gaff
sails eliminated yardarms, with the result that weight aloft was reduced, which in turn
reduced the requirements in ballasting and therefore reduced displacement and wetted
surface. Gaff rigs are more powerful to weather than square rigs, and gaff rigs require
less manpower because they can be controlled entirely from the deck. Though the large,
transoceanic ships continued to use square rigging until the end, many medium-size
ships after 1600 were partially or entirely gaff-rigged. At the top is a "schooner," a
type very popular in colonial America. At center left is a "sloop," popular on smaller
boats. The other three vessels are compromises between gaff rigging and square rig-
ging. Center right is a "hermaphrodite brig," at bottom left is a "barkentine," and at
bottom right is a "bark."

Americans, until after World War I, put a lot of sail on their vessels. On schooners, the boom of the aftermost sail extended far past the stern rail, and the head sail invariably was on a stay that ran to a bowsprit, far overboard of the bow.

Clipper ships were the epitome of stacking canvas on square-riggers. In addition to spankers and a dozen or more studding sails and staysails, the last of the clippers carried square sails six high on three different masts.

The reason for the large sail plans on this side of the Atlantic is that Americans, from the beginning, have tended to design for average conditions of weather. Europeans, on the other hand, designed for extreme conditions, and their sail areas tended to be smaller. For runs to the West Indies, the most common passage for American smugglers, the average conditions were light to moderate winds.

With all sails set, American schooners moved along well in light air and reached hull speed[1] in moderate wind. If the wind became stronger, sail had to be reduced, because the sails began developing power that the hulls couldn't handle. The excess power, which had no release through an increase in speed, was a threat. It made the boat less controllable and it threatened damage to the rigging.

Beginning about 1900, sailing craft began to appear that blew the hull-speed formula to pieces, but that is a topic for later chapters. Yachting in the late 1800's operated within the hull-speed formula, and some yachting circles today (most ocean racing and the America's Cup races, for instance) that are tied to heavy-displacement hulls must still operate within it. In these circles, the objective is faster acceleration to hull speed and designing rigs to reach hull speed in lighter and lighter air.

Reaching hull speed in light air is a two-part thing. The first part is power, which concerns the rigging, and the second part is resistance, which concerns the hull. In closed-course races, where marks must be rounded frequently, one might also add a third part, handiness, which concerns

---

[1]The formula here is: $1.25 \times \sqrt{LWL} =$ hull speed. LWL is length on the waterline (in feet), and hull speed is the theoretical maximum in knots. According to the formula a hull of 36 feet LWL can go no faster than 7.5 knots, a hull of 100 feet no faster than 12.5 knots. The formula is fairly accurate for old-time vessels today whose hulls are of the deep-displacement type. The formula was probably worked out, originally, from observation. The modern, scientific explanation has to do with the building up of the bow wave and the quarter wave. At or near the hull speed, according to the explanation, these two waves begin operating in tandem and cause a great hollow (and therefore suction) at the stern. In the final days of commercial sailing and the early days of yachting, hull speed was a very real limitation. On many types of boats today (scows, trimarans, catamarans, etc.) the formula is meaningless. In fact, the formula would have been meaningless to Polynesians of a thousand years ago. At that time, they were sailing catamarans far above "hull speed."

hardware for handling lines to set sails. This third part, though critical in closed courses, is of far less importance in ocean racing, where points of sailing are infrequently changed.

Increasing power of sail, up through World War I, was mostly a matter of figuring ways to put up and to handle more and more sail. Before then, there were few dramatic improvements in rigging, except to make it bigger. However, there were two significant developments: the introduction of cotton sailcloth in the early 1800's, and the sewing of sails so that seams were parallel, rather than perpendicular, to the flow of the air.

Before 1800, linen was used as sailcloth. Linen has a lot of stretch, which doesn't matter much for square-riggers but is a definite aerodynamic disadvantage for fore-and-afters. Linen also "leaks" air through its loose weave, and that is a disadvantage to either type of rig.

Hand-woven cotton sails appeared in the first decade of the 1800's, but they were not widely accepted at first, party because they were very expensive. During the War of 1812, ships of both the United States and England were still carrying linen sails. At that time, in light air, it was common practice to haul buckets of water aloft to dampen the linen, thereby shrinking the weave and cutting down on the leakage of air.

Cotton sails leaked less and held their shape far better than linen. Many privateers of the War of 1812 used cotton, and it was generally conceded that vessels with cotton sails, all else being equal, were faster.

By about 1830, the introduction of the power loom made cotton cheap enough so that it was competitive with linen; and the power loom also improved cotton as a sailcloth because the fibers could be woven much tighter than they ever were woven by hand. The tight weaving reduced the leakage almost to zero, and it also resulted in sails that would fairly well hold the shape to which they were sewn. This quality of cotton became especially important in the 1900's when the science of aerodynamics was applied to sail design.

Seaming sails horizontally, parallel with air flow, was the invention of Nathanael G. Herreshoff. The horizontal sewing increased power because it cut down the interruption in the flow of air across the sail.

The matter of resistance to reaching hull speed is a complicated subject, mainly because resistance is not the only factor a designer must consider when laying down the lines of a hull. If it were, all hulls, below the waterline, would be approximately the shape of half a fish, cut lengthwise. Such a shape would have the least resistance to water.

However, in designing a sailing hull, the designer must consider steering, lateral resistance (the thing that keeps the hull from slipping sideways when power is not directly in line with the desired direction of travel—and that's most of the time, in a sailboat), righting moment (a factor involving the interrelation of the center of gravity and the center of buoyancy, which keeps the hull from turning onto its side, and the effect that waves have on everything else.

But for a moment, let us consider hull design only in regard to resistance. The terms we must use are "wetted surface" and "fluid flow."

A solid object passing through water is hampered by friction, and the friction is between the water and the surface of the object. If the speed remained the same, and the object remained the same proportionate shape, but became larger, friction would increase as the area of the surface (wetted surface).

Now suppose the object is a proposed boat hull—or rather, the portion of the hull that is going to be below the waterline. Assume the displacement will be 5 tons. We are talking, of course, only about displacement hulls, which remain at a constant draft, and not about planing hulls. Into what shape can we mold the bottom to present the least amount of surface to the water around it? The answer is a sphere, completely submerged.

Of course a sphere is an absurdity as a shape for a boat bottom, but one thing we know is what wetted surface will increase (though displacement remains constant) the more we depart from the shape of a sphere.

The nearest thing to a sphere that would be remotely practical as a configuration for a boat bottom is, perhaps, a hemisphere (flat side up). For least wetted surface, this would beat anything except something nearer to a sphere.

Fluid flow around a hemisphere is not smooth, however, so it is necessary to compromise wetted surface further to obtain a fluid-dynamic shape. This is simply a matter of drawing out the hemisphere into an oblong shape. The precise shape is not a subject within the scope of this book, so let us just say that the shape would closely resemble the bottom half of a rainbow trout or a salmon, minus fins, tail, and gills.

With the hypothetical displacement of 5 tons, the whole problem of fluid flow can be visualized as follows: Every time the boat moves its own length, it must take apart and put back together 5 tons of water. The trick is to move this mass of water no more than is necessary, and the best way is to move it out at right angles to the path of the hull, and back in, also at right angles. In addition, the acceleration and deceleration of the mass along these right angles should be even. If one imagines a fish passing through water, and then thinks of the motion of the water only as motion at right angles to the fish's line of travel, it may help in visualizing the desired effect.

The idea of building ship bottoms to the general shape of fish goes back a long way. Drawings of designers five and six centuries ago occasionally have sketches of fish superimposed on sketches of hulls. Though designers today are not apt to put an overlay of a fish on their blueprints, their science of fluid dynamics leads them still to shapes approximating those of fish.

Up through the commercial sailing era, ship underbodies resembled the fish configuration, but with something extra added. The extra was a long, straight keel. Though hulls were rounded smoothly, fore and aft and up and down, the planking was also built down to this keel.

The long keel probably hurt fluid flow very little, but it did increase wetted surface considerably. Still, this modification of the fish configuration was necessary to reduce leeway. It increased lateral resistance.

The Americans, though they built long, thin hulls, still used the long keels. In the early 1800's, certain builders began putting in a protruding keel, a heavy board on edge that protruded below the planking all along the bottom of the hull. This was simply a matter of letting the keelboard stick out below the point of the lowest plank, and part of the keel thus became, in effect, a long fin that ran the length of the bottom. The schooner yacht *America* had such a fixture on her bottom. The obvious advantage is that a greater area of lateral resistance is afforded so that deadrise can be reduced and beam can be slightly increased. The extra beam would make the hull somewhat stiffer[2] and power would be increased, especially in working to weather.

Through the 1700's and early 1800's, keels were gradually shortened, lengthwise, and hull design began moving in the direction of what we now call "cutaway ends." In other words, they began moving more toward the fish shape.

This cutting away of ends reduces lateral resistance and therefore increases leeway, but this problem was solved for a lot of boats with the invention of the centerboard.

The centerboard came into common use in the United States in the first half of the nineteenth century, and it became practically standard equipment on all sloops and schooners operating in coastal waters, in rivers, and on the Great Lakes. During the lumbering boom of the 1800's, nearly every sailing vessel in the Great Lakes was rigged with a centerboard, or drop keel, as it was called then.

The centerboard is simply a fin that can be lowered into the water, right through the bottom of the boat. Like centerboards on sailboats today, a cabinet was built up from the hole to a level higher than the waterline,

---

[2] "Tenderness" and "stiffness" are opposites. A boat is said to be tender if it has little resistance to heeling. It is said to be stiff if it has great resistance to heeling. Hulls that are of wide beam are generally very stiff, while narrow hulls are generally tender, especially in low angles of heel, though if they are heavily ballasted they become progressively stiffer as the angle of heel is increased.

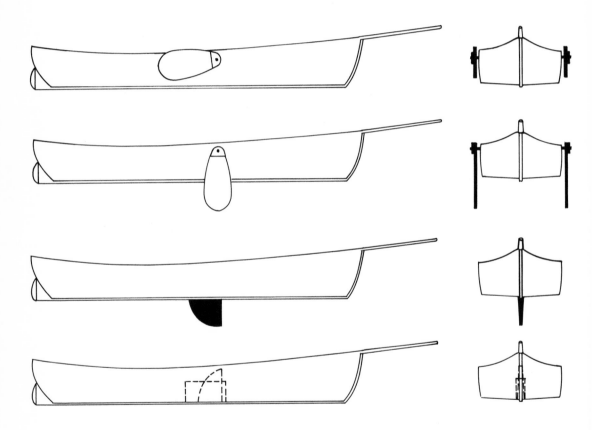

RETRACTABLE LATERAL RESISTANCE. Vessels of shallow draft, unless they are sailing with the wind, will not stay on track very well unless they have some type of fin along the bottom. The Northmen, and many others afterward, built their boats with protruding keels, a type of permanent fin. However, in vessels that must operate at times in shallow water, it was necessary that fins be retractable. The Dutch, who operate out of shallow canals, invented leeboards, shown retracted in the top drawing and down in the second drawing. The leeboards hang at the side of the boat and are hauled up or let down by lanyards. The centerboard, shown in the down position in the third drawing and retracted in the bottom drawing, became popular in America in the early 1800's. The board operates through a slot in the hull.

but in the 1800's it was much more difficult to seal the base of these cabinets to the bottom of the hull than it is with today's methods. In the 1800's some of the centerboards went through a notch in a plank beside the keel.

The centerboard solves all problems of leeway, and the rest of an underbody can be molded without regard to it. The reason centerboarders became so popular on rivers and coastal waters is that the board, being retractable, enables the boat to operate in shallow waters. For a commercial vessel, the centerboard hull has another advantage in that there is a lot of lateral resistance even when the hull is empty and riding high.

Centerboards were apparently something new in the early 1800's, but the idea of a retractable fin was not. A century or two before, the Dutch began using leeboards, a pair of fins that swung up and down from pins at the rail, one on either side of the boat. These Dutch craft were flat-bottomed and of shallow draft because they had to operate in shallow canals on the way out and the way back in from sea. When in deep water, the leeboards were lowered. They extended well below the bottom of the hull. Centerboards operate exactly the same way except that they operate through a hole in the center of the hull.

Occasionally, even today, you see a sailing boat with leeboards. They are still quite common in the Netherlands, but for some reason they never caught on in other parts of the world. The most common application of leeboards in the United States today is on canoes. A canoe rigged with a sail will invariably have leeboards to provide lateral resistance.

The use of a fin (centerboard, leeboards, or nonretractable fin) frees a designer to follow the fish form and lay out a hull with more consideration for fluid flow and wetted surface. Many sailboats of the 1880's and 1890's had underbodies that were basically fish-shaped, but with fins protruding from or through the bottom. Such configurations are very popular today.

One thing that cannot be ignored in hull design, fin or no fin, is stability. We touched on this subject earlier in discussing weight distribution and the effect it had on the center of gravity. But center of gravity (CG) is only one of the factors of stability. The other factor is center of buoyancy (CB).

In any vessel, the CG is that point at which it is balanced in all directions. If the boat were floating in space and then someone spun it, in any direction, it would rotate around the CG. The CG never shifts within a boat unless weight is redistributed.

When a boat is in water, gravity pulls it downward. If the weight of the boat is 5 tons, the gravity exerts a force of 5 tons and one may view this force as being straight down along a vertical line that passes through the CG. Straight down means straight down with respect to the earth, *not* with respect to the boat. It matters not if the boat is heeled to one side or the

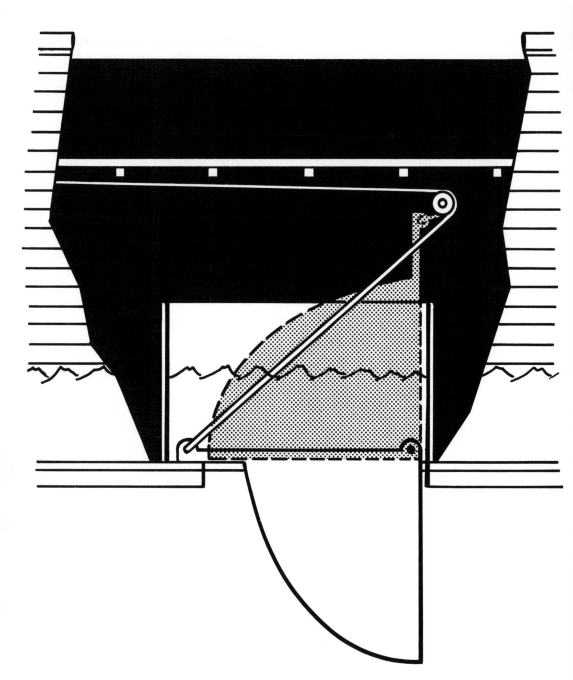

WATERTIGHT WELL. One of the biggest problems, before modern materials were used to build boats, was making the centerboard well watertight. The slot in the keel through which the centerboard passes is surrounded by a narrow, boxlike enclosure built up higher than the vessel's waterline. The inside of the enclosure is constantly filled with water to the same height as the water on the outside of the hull. Centerboards were used on many large vessels, particularly on the Great Lakes, in the 1800's. Early builders of centerboarders had difficulty in making and maintaining a tight seal between the bottom of the box enclosure and the bottom of the hull.

other, or is down at the bow or the stern. Put the boat in any position you like—60 degrees over or knocked flat or upside down—and the gravity is still pulling straight down through the CG.

Buoyancy, of course, is the counterforce to gravity. Buoyancy is water pressure pushing up on the hull, and if gravity is pulling the hull downward with a force of 5 tons, then buoyancy is pushing it upward with a force of 5 tons. All of the force of buoyancy may be viewed as operating on a central point within the hull, and this point is called the center of buoyancy. And all the force may be said to operate straight up along a vertical line through the CB—straight up with respect to the earth, *not* with respect to the boat.

Now if you take a boat that is setting perfectly still on a day without wind and in water without waves, the boat will be setting upright and the vertical lines through the CG and the CB will be one and the same. Suppose you could take the mast in your fingers and tip it to one side, then let it go. The boat would rock a few times, but it would soon settle back to an upright position.

What has happened is that you have moved the center of buoyancy to the side to which you tipped the boat. But the center of gravity remained in the same place. The CB had moved away from the CG. And when you let go the mast, the force acting through the CB pushed the low side up, working against the CG, which pushed the high side down. When the boat had settled back to an upright position, the CG and the CB had realigned themselves.

We have established that the CB moves within the hull, while the CG does not. Is there any way of expressing the nature of the CB's movement? Yes. The center of buoyancy is always at the volumetric center of the displacement of the hull.

Take the boat from the example above, put it in any position you like, and then imagine that the water freezes. Pull the boat out and there will be a hole in the ice where the hull was. This hole is the displacement of the hull, and the center of the volume of this hole is the CB for that position of the boat. Obviously the shape of the hole will change for every angle of the hull; therefore the CB moves with every change of angle of the hull.

Of course there is an exception to all this: a hull with a perfectly round bottom. With such a bottom, the shape of the hole would always be the same, regardless of the position of the hull, and of course the CB would not move. That is why round-bottom boats are unstable—a canoe, for instance. Canoe bottoms are not perfectly rounded, but they come fairly close.

A rowboat, on the other hand, with a wide, flat bottom and sharp, angular bilges to near-vertical sides, tends to be very stiff. Tip a rowboat even slightly to one side and the sharp bilge moves down into the water as the bilge on the other comes to the surface. The CB moves instantly well over to the low side, creating tremendous righting arm.[3]

For such stability, the penalty is, of course, resistance and therefore decreased speed. A rowboat-type hull has several times the wetted surface and a much less smooth fluid flow than a canoe of approximately the same capacity.

It may appear from these two extreme examples—rowboat vs. canoe—that one cannot have it both ways, that low resistance and high stability are incompatible. This is somewhat true, but a lot of things have happened, many of them in the last hundred years, to bring stability and low resistance together in the same vessel.

One thing that improves stability, as we have already mentioned, is getting weight down low, or in other words lowering the CG. As was mentioned earlier, square-riggers had the problem of heavy rigging, requiring heavy ballasting as a counterweight, which increased displacement and therefore increased wetted surface.

The French, in years gone by, were always fond of designs with low centers of gravity. During their centuries of war with England, they occasionally captured an English warship, and of course the English captured some of theirs. When either side captured a ship, it usually put the vessel into service in its own navy.

Along toward the last of the rivalry, the English ships were very heavily armed. They often had three and sometimes four decks, all bristling with heavy cannon. When the French got hold of one of these vessels, they very often altered it to make its center of gravity lower. Upon capturing a three- or four-deck vessel, they would run it into a shipyard, remove the guns from the upper deck, and then cut the whole ship down by one deck before putting it back into service. The French were quite willing to sacrifice some firepower to gain stiffness, speed, and maneuverability.

On smaller vessels, the Americans went a long way in bringing down centers of gravity with their fore-and-aft rigs and low-profile hulls.

The biggest breakthrough in stability, however, was the introduction of outside ballasting and its eventual evolution to the uncapsizable hull.

Earlier in this chapter we explained that it takes 100 pounds 10 feet below the CG to counter 100 pounds 10 feet above the CG, and 1,000

---

[3]Righting arm is the horizontal distance between the CB and the CG. If the force of buoyancy is 5 tons, then righting moment is 5 foot-tons if the centers are 1 foot apart horizontally, 10 foot-tons if the centers are 2 feet apart, and so on. In other words, righting moment is the product of the force of buoyancy (a constant) and the length of the righting arm (a variable). When the boat is upright, there is no righting moment because the centers are vertically aligned and the variable is zero.

pounds 10 feet below the CG to counter 100 pounds at 100 feet above the CG, and so on. In that discussion it was assumed that 10 feet was the very bottom of the bilge and that ballast could be placed no farther below the CG than that.

But suppose you weighed all of this ballast and then had a foundry cast that weight in iron or lead to a shape that could be bolted along the bottom of the keel, *outside* the hull. Assume that the gain in depth of the ballast is 2 feet. Then the ballast would have 12 feet of leverage, rather than 10, and the boat would either become more stable or the amount (weight) of the ballast could be reduced by one-fifth. Because just as the weight of a yardarm has more effect as it is raised farther and farther aloft, the weight of ballast has more effect as it is placed farther and farther down.

The English were the first to put outside ballast on ships. Two schooners were built for the Admiralty in 1796 with short sections of pig iron bolted along their keels. The schooners were designed by Samuel Bentham, and in addition to the innovation in ballast, they also had other new features, such as iron windlasses and winches and geared steering.

Neither vessel was particularly successful, and outside ballasting never caught on in commercial or naval warships. The gears and the winches caught on, however, and such devices regularly replaced rope-tackle steering mechanisms and capstans on sailing ships built afterward.

Deep ballasting did catch on in yachting, and it was designed into many yachts, both large and small, along toward the end of the nineteenth century. It first appeared on the America's Cup defenders in designs by Edward Burgess, the Boston designer of the 1880's. From deeper and deeper ballasting, the uncapsizable hull evolved.

The whole trick to building a sailboat that is uncapsizable is to get the center of gravity below the center of buoyancy. Recall for an instant the discussion of the rowboat (flat-bottom) and the way the center of buoyancy moves to the low side when the boat is heeled. Now suppose that there is an iron fin running three feet deep beneath the keel of this rowboat and that there is a heavy weight welded to the very bottom of this fin. Further suppose that this weight is heavy enough so that the CG of the total boat is 2 feet under the water. Where does the CG go when the boat is heeled?

As we have said before, it stays in the same place, with respect to the boat. But with respect to the vertical of the earth, it moves over beneath the high side of the boat. In other words, the CG and the center of buoyancy move in opposite directions. And the greater the angle of heel, the farther the CB and CG move apart, creating even more leverage to pull the hull back upright. Even if the boat were upside down, with the CG perfectly aligned over the CB, the very slightest nudge to misalign the two

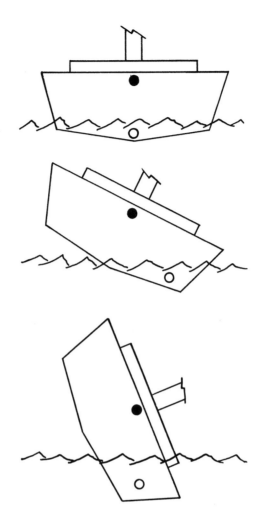

● CENTER OF GRAVITY
○ CENTER OF BUOYANCY

STABILITY—UNBALLASTED HULL. Unballasted hulls are necessarily of the flat-bottom or shallow-V type. The center of gravity is above the center of buoyancy, and, as in the top drawing, they are vertically aligned when the hull is perfectly upright. At only a slight angle of heel, as in the middle drawing, the center of buoyancy moves far over to the low side. The force of buoyancy is pushing up and the force of gravity is pulling down through the respective centers, and because the forces are greatly separated horizontally, the leverage between the two is very powerful. At high angles of heel, as in the bottom drawing, the leverage is not nearly so great because the horizontal distance between the centers is becoming shorter. As soon as the center of gravity moves over the center of buoyancy, the hull capsizes. Hulls of this type have great resistance to capsizing at low angles of heel, but the resistance becomes less and less as the angle increases.

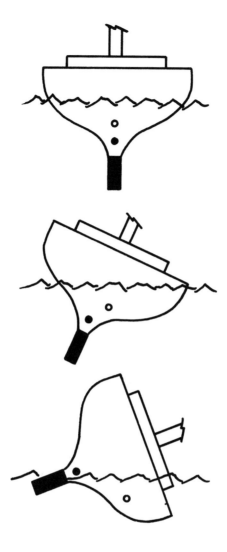

● CENTER OF GRAVITY
○ CENTER OF BUOYANCY

STABILITY—BALLASTED HULLS. Ballasted hulls in which the center of gravity is below the center of buoyancy are "uncapsizable." The more the hull heels, the farther apart the center of gravity and the center of buoyancy become. Even if the hull were completely upside down, the center of gravity would be above the center of buoyancy and the hull would turn itself back upright. Such hulls have very little resistance, however, to low angles of heel, as in the middle drawing, though they develop more and more resistance at greater and greater angles of heel. Unlike flat-bottom, unballasted hulls, which sail well upright even in stiff wind, most ballasted hulls are designed to sail while heeled. A flat-bottom, deep-ballasted hull, such as Herreshoff's Dilemma (described in the next chapter), can be both uncapsizable and capable of sailing stiffly upright.

centers would cause the boat instantly to flop back upright. (For the sake of this example, think of the rowboat as completely decked and with all hatches closed.)

Of course a rowboat-type hull with a weighted keel would be tremendously stiff. Because the horizontal distance between the CG and the CB would build up so fast, the slightest angle of heel would give the two opposing forces tremendous leverage to right the boat.

Now let us go to the other extreme by taking the weighted iron fin off the rowboat-type hull and putting it on a canoe-type hull (also a hypothetical decked vessel). The canoe would then be uncapsizable, just like the rowboat, but the canoe, instead of being stiff, would be very tender. In other words, it would have little righting moment at low angles of heel, but the righting force would build up as the angle of heel increased.

The reason for the tenderness is that on round bottoms, the center of buoyancy moves very little toward the low side. The lever arm between CB and CG, in the case of the canoe, is increased mostly by the moving of the CG toward the high side. At low angles of heel, this distance is not building up very fast. At steep angles of heel, a powerful righting moment builds because the two centers are far apart.

Modern keel yachts are generally somewhere between the two extremes, neither hard bilges (as the rowboat-type) nor uniformly rounded bilges. Hot racing boats generally have higher initial stability, so that they will sail more nearly upright (and therefore develop more power in the sails). Cruising sailboats, on the other hand, will generally be more tender, so that the rolling motion in seas will be less jerky. With less stiffness, the boat will not be quite as fast as it might have been, but it will be much more comfortable.

III Sailboats for Pleasure

Science and industrialization, which brought automobiles, airplanes, and motor vessels to the world, also brought changes to sailing vessels, in two different ways.

First, because motor ships began carrying the cargo of merchants and the guns of navies, sailing vessels became things only for sport. The very form of sailing vessels changed from that of solid workhorses to high-speed thoroughbreds.

Second, the details of sailing vessels changed because the forging, casting, and machining of metal made possible a multitude of new parts, fittings, and methods of construction that would have been unthinkable a few decades earlier.

The first high-powered sailing machine to become famous in the United States was the yacht *America*, built in 1851. The *America* was not modern. She was a wooden vessel, and in both form and detail she was a close copy of New York pilot schooners. She was a very advanced boat for the old era, but nonetheless was of the old era. The *America* brought the One

Hundred Guineas Cup (now the America's Cup) to the New York Yacht Club by winning a race in England, mostly on her extraordinary ability in light air and to weather.

The death of George Steers, designer of the *America*, in 1856 left a sort of vacuum in sailing design, and there was little interest in yachting until after the U. S. Civil War. But when the war was over the era of modern yachting, the era of the sailing machine, began.

Four men dominated the field of yacht design during the fifty years that began about 1870, and it may be said of them that they led yachting into the era of science and industrialization. They were A. Cary Smith, Edward Burgess, William Gardner, and Nathanael G. Herreshoff.

A. Cary Smith was born in 1837 in Chelsea Village, which was then out in the country but is now part of New York City. As a boy, Smith spent a lot of time with other boys sailing model yachts. When Smith was fourteen, his father, a Presbyterian minister, took him over to a shipyard on East 12th Street to have a look at the *America* while she was under construction. Four years later, instead of going to college, he went to work for a boatyard in New Jersey. While there, he did a lot of planking, caulking, and sailing and a little bit of designing. He also hired a retired shipbuilder to teach him drafting.

In 1867, after Smith had gone into business for himself back over in New York, he helped design the 62-foot cutter *Vindex*, which was probably the first iron yacht built in the United States.

Early in his career, Smith designed dozens of successful sloops and schooners, among them another iron sloop, *Mischief*, defender of the America's Cup in 1881. However, Smith and his firm were not strictly yacht designers, but rather all-around naval architects. He also designed steam yachts, and in 1889 he got a commission to draw up a commercial steamship for the New Haven Steamboat Line. The drawings became the 300-foot *Richard Peck*, and in her, Smith's experience in laying down yacht hulls paid off handsomely. On her trial run, the *Peck's* sleek hull cut through the water at over 20 miles per hour while burning only about half the coal per mile as the next best ship of the New Haven line.

Smith was one of the first designers to start with drawings instead of models. At the height of his career, there raged the controversy of cutter vs. sloop.[1] Proponents of each type were vigorously antagonistic to the

---

[1] "Sloop" in this context of the 1880's does not mean what it commonly does today—a boat with a single mast that is fore-and-aft rigged. At this period in the argument of sloop vs. cuttter, a sloop was a boat of broad beam and extremely shallow draft that is unballasted and has a retractable centerboard. Coincidentally, it was sloop-rigged. A cutter, by contrast, was a boat of narrow beam, deeply and heavily ballasted. The cutter also was sloop-rigged, or if one wishes to split hairs, cutter-rigged, which is different from the sloop rig only in a few slight details. The sloop was generally con-

other, but Smith never threw in with either faction. He was a strict prag-
matist who went his own way in designing, with the usual results somewhere between the two popular extremes. Many of his vessels were the
so-called "compromise hulls," which have both ballasting and centerboards,
the centerboards not only providing lateral resistance, but also serving as
trim tabs to balance helm on different points of sailing, by manipulating
the board to change the center of lateral resistance. Smith is closely iden-
tified with this type of hull.

Though Smith, himself a yachtsman and sailing enthusiast, never gave
up the designing of yachts, his firm was moving more and more toward
steam and motor-vessel design at the time of his death in 1911.

Edward Burgess, with whom Smith was always on friendly terms, was
the designer of three America's Cup defenders, one each for challenges in
1885, 1886, and 1887.

Burgess was born of a wealthy family in Sandwich, Massachusetts, in
1848. As a boy he was interested in sailing and spent many summers in
formal races. However, when he went to Harvard, he studied and then
lectured in entomology. In the summer of 1883 he was in England, where
he studied yachts and compared them with American types. This was at
the height of the cutter-sloop controversy, and it is said of Burgess that he
admired the safety and weatherliness of the English types, but disliked
their narrowness and extreme angles of heel.

Family financial reversals forced Burgess to turn to earning his own
living, and in 1884, he and a brother set up an office in Boston to design and
sell yachts. The business did so poorly at first that the brother dropped
out, leaving Edward alone. He struggled along for nearly a year and then
some way or other was chosen to design a candidate for defense of the
America's Cup.

The result was a compromise sloop, *Puritan*, the first America's Cup
boat with outside ballast. *Puritan*, built by a Boston syndicate, beat the
New York boats in trials and went on to beat the British challenger.

Puritan made Burgess famous, and he went on to design two more Cup
defenders, the third of which, *Volunteer*, was the first defender with a
steel hull.

Burgess also did considerable work on 30, 40 and 46 class boats, the last
of which were just beginning their first season of racing when Burgess
fell ill with typhoid fever and died on July 31, 1891, at the age of forty-
three. He had been a professional naval architect for only seven years. In
all, he designed 137 boats, most of them sailing yachts.

---

sidered an American type, the cutter an English type. The cutter, of course, was uncapsizable but had low initial stability; the sloop had high initial stability, but was
capsizable.

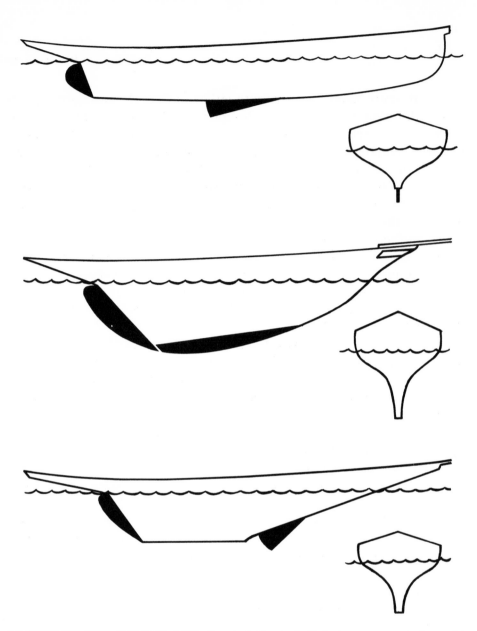

YACHTS OF THE GOLDEN AGE. Great strides in hull design were made in yachts built in the late 1800's. Puritan *(top), an America's Cup Defender by Edward Burgess in 1885, had a centerboard and such forward-looking features as outside ballast along her keel, but her general configuration below water was very bulky, an influence, no doubt, from designs of commercial sailing vessels.* Liris *(center), a design by William Gardner in 1889, was one of the first sailing hulls of the modern type. Her hull was deep and thin and she carried her ballast far below the center of gravity, giving her the leverage to handle a tremendously large sail plan.* Elmina *(bottom), a schooner of 1901 by A. Cary Smith, was less extreme in draft and thinness. Note that the centerboard, as it is lowered, will cause the center of lateral resistance to move forward, helping the boat to head up to weather with little or no cock in the rudder. (These boats are not drawn to the same scale.)*

William Gardner, of New York City, was the first naval architect in the United States to prepare himself with a formal theoretical and technical education. He was born in Oswego, New York, a shipping port at the Lake Ontario entrance to the Erie Canal, in 1859. Little is known of his life as a boy except that his parents were well-to-do and that he traveled with them a lot, often at sea.

Gardner graduated from Cornell University about 1880, worked for a time for practical experience in shipyards, and then in 1884 went to England, where he obtained permission to study at the Royal Naval College at Greenwich. After completing his studies there, he spent two more years in shipyards, at Tyne and on the Clyde. In 1888 he opened his office in New York.

One of the first boats Gardner designed, and the one that established his reputation, was for the 40-foot class (40 feet at the waterline). She was the *Liris,* built in 1889. In laying down her lines, Gardner used his technical expertise to shave every last ounce off the hull and the spars while leaving the strength to swing a deep-going keel of 16 tons of lead. The result was an extremely powerful vessel. It carried 3,600 square feet of sail while the usual sail area in the 40-footers was 3,200 to 3,300.

The *Liris* was a very successful boat, and her design was the pattern for all of Gardner's boats, namely to engineer them for the lowest possible weight so that they could carry the largest possible sail plan. He did not often depart from tradition, but he was capable of carrying tradition to technical extremes.

It was Gardner who designed the famous *Atlantic,* a three-masted centerboard schooner, 185 feet overall. The *Atlantic* was built in 1903 and proceeded to win a number of races. In 1905, in a race for a cup put up by the German Emperor, the *Atlantic* won by setting a record for transatlantic passage (Sandy Hook, New Jersey, to Falmouth, England) of just over eleven days and sixteen hours. The record still stands.

None of Gardner's boats ever defended the America's Cup, and in fact he designed only one candidate, the *Vanitie,* for a challenge in 1914. Trials were held in 1914, but because of World War I, the boats were then laid up until 1920, when new trials were held. In trials both before and after the war, *Vanitie* and a Herreshoff candidate, *Resolute,* were so closely matched that there was little to choose between and *Resolute* was eventually selected, perhaps partly because Herreshoff had designed all five of the previous Cup defenders.

Because of eye trouble, Gardner retired from his firm in 1925, five years before there was another America's Cup challenge. On May 7, 1934, he died at his home at Bay Head, New Jersey.

Nathanael G. Herreshoff, whose boats won six straight America's Cup races between 1893 and 1920, stands out above all his contemporaries. Smith, Burgess, and Gardner were all praiseworthy designers, but Herreshoff, much more than any of them, adopted the methods of science and industry, applied them to the sailing machine, and brought yachting into the modern age. He was an inventor who did more than any other man to make sailboats what they are today.

One of the reasons for Herreshoff's tremendous success was that he was not only a designer. He also was a builder, a builder in the broadest sense in that his firm not only put his boats together, but fabricated most if not all of the parts that went into them, right down to the turnbuckles and cleats.

Herreshoff was born on March 18, 1848 near Bristol, Rhode Island, an old seaport and shipbuilding town. Everywhere around him, as he grew up, were hundreds of expert craftsmen of the shipping trades. The boy's father, a man of leisure, dabbled in the building and sailing of small boats.

Herreshoff was educated as an engineer at the Massachusetts Institute of Technology and went to work for a steam-engine manufacturer in Providence. In 1878 he joined his brother, John, who was blind, at the Herreshoff Manufacturing Co., in Bristol.

When Nathanael came into the business, most of the work at the plant, on Bristol's waterfront, was in steam-driven craft. The Herreshoffs had always kept themselves in sailboats and they occasionally took an order for one, but for over ten years after Nathanael joined the firm, the main business was in steam yachts, launches, and commercial vessels and in steam-driven torpedo boats for the U. S. Navy. Herreshoff Manufacturing, because it built its own engines, had a well-equipped foundry and machine shop. All the tools and organization of modern industry were at Nathanael's fingertips, under his control, when *Gloriana* went down the ways in the spring of '91.

If one were to choose the yacht that put sailing into the twentieth century, it would have to be *Gloriana*. There is no other choice. There has been no really dramatic improvement in keelboats since she was built.

Gloriana was designed and built by Herreshoff in the fall and winter of 1890 for Commodore E. D. Morgan of the New York Yacht Club. She was for a new, 46-foot class (46 feet on the waterline) that began racing in the summer of 1891. There were nineteen of the boats in the fleet that year, several of them designed by Burgess, others by Smith and Gardner. *Gloriana* won every race in the class that summer—which would have been quite an achievement in ordinary circumstances, but was all the more so because the class as a whole was considerably faster than previous boats of comparable size.

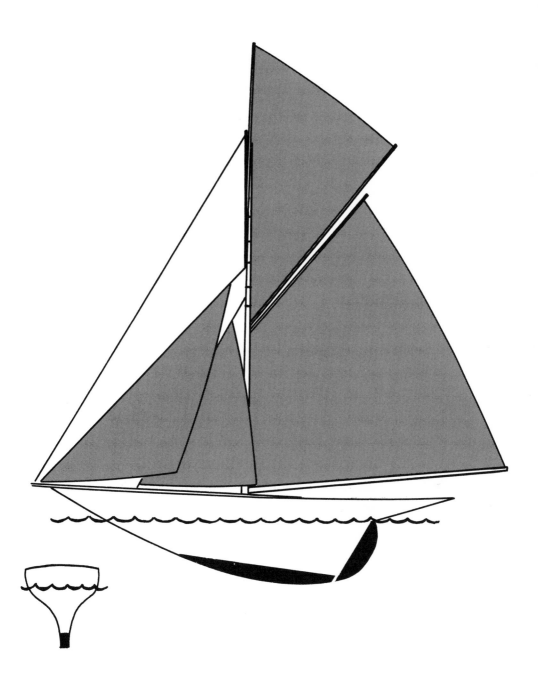

GLORIANA. Few fundamental improvements have been made in the design of mono-hulls since Gloriana, designed and built by Nathanael G. Herreshoff in 1890-91. Her basic features are similar to, though not as extreme as, those of Liris. Gloriana was deeply ballasted, which enabled her to carry a large amount of sail without a great penalty in weight and wetted surface. Her hull was designed so that her waterline length (and therefore her potential for speed) increased as she heeled. Herreshoff literally designed her to sail somewhat on her side.

In *Gloriana*, Herreshoff made several bold departures. While only 46 feet long on the water, she was 70 feet overall, leaving her with tremendous overhangs. From the bow, her stem swept aft to a curved outside keel of lead. The underline of her stern swept in several feet to the rudder post before it went into the water.

These long overhangs kept *Gloriana's* measured length within the class, but at the same time provided a platform for a very powerful rig. When *Gloriana* heeled, the sides of her overhangs went more and more into the water, giving her a lot of reserve buoyance that both stabilized the platform, kept her more nearly upright, and *increased her waterline length*. This last factor enabled her to exceed the theoretical hull speed for 46 feet.

Up to a certain angle of heel, *Gloriana's* wetted surface decreased and fluid flow improved. Herreshoff literally had designed her to sail somewhat on her sides.

The hull form, more than anything else, is what made *Gloriana* fast, but there were other features that contributed to her speed.

The hull was of an unusual construction that was both light and strong, a tribute to Herreshoff's ability as an engineer. Double planking was laid over steel frames and fastened with screws. The outer planking was laid with white lead, but with no caulking between the seams, which made a much smoother surface than was usual in those days.

Hardware, all fabricated by Herreshoff, was tailor-made for *Gloriana*, and there was not a wasted ounce in any of it. Contrary to the usual practice of designing hulls and then putting on rigging and sails as a separate matter, Herreshoff engineered *Gloriana* as one unit, carefully providing for a light and sturdy, though gigantic, rig. The engineering paid off, for the rigging failed on many of the 46-footers in 1891, but *Gloriana* was out the whole summer without ever seeing the inside of a yard.

Gloriana, though she revolutionized yacht design, was no stopping place for Herreshoff. While she was out on the circuit in the summer of '91, Herreshoff himself was home building yet another boat that was to have a tremendous influence on smaller racing craft. The boat was *Dilemma*. She was the first fin-keeler.

The body of *Dilemma* was very shallow, shaped something like a long, narrow dish. She was 38 feet overall, 20 feet on the waterline and 7 feet in the beam. Fastened to her bottom was a metal plate, about 9 feet long, and 4 or 5 feet deep. At the bottom of this plate was a cigar-shaped bulb of 2 tons of lead.

Though *Dilemma* did not race, and there is little to compare her with for performance, many of her type have come along since, enabling us to tell her general characteristics. She had a very low center of gravity and because of this she could carry a very powerful (large) sail plan for her

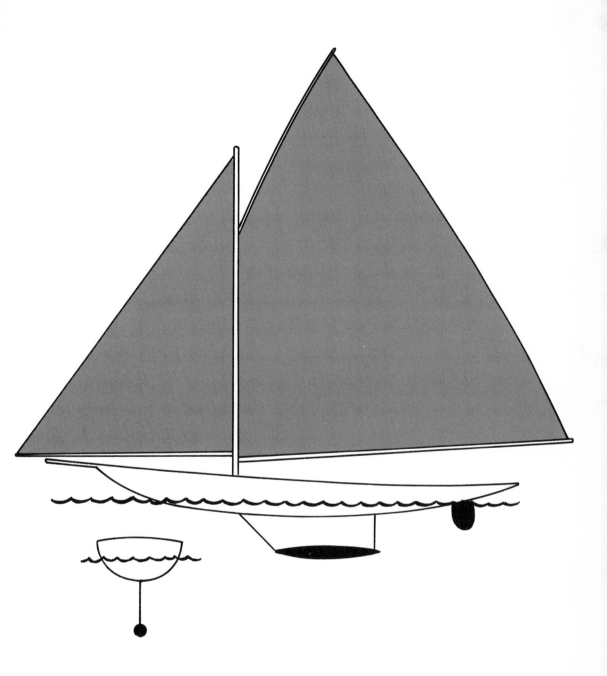

DILEMMA—BREAKTHROUGH IN BALLASTING. Fin keels are so common today that it seems they have been around forever. Actually, the first one appeared on Dilemma, an experimental boat built by Herreshoff in 1891. The cigar-shaped bulb on the bottom is solid lead. Connecting it to the hull is a steel plate. The advantage of this arrangement is that the ballast is concentrated at a very deep level, far away from the center of buoyancy. The ballast is acting through a long lever arm and therefore has more force. The greater efficiency in ballasting can be used either to decrease the amount of ballast or to increase sail area.

displacement. Partly because of her shape, and partly because of her light displacement (light with respect to her size and to the size of her sail plan), she had relatively little wetted surface. Because of her scowlike hull, she did not do very well in a sea, but was very, very fast in relatively calm water. Because of her spade rudder (separate from and set back several feet from the plate), she was easy to steer. The rudder, being a long way from the turning axis, had a lot of leverage. Finally, because of her light displacement and the dishlike shape of her hull, she had little room for accommodations.

Dilemma probably was the inspiration behind the *Newport 30's*, a one-design class by Herreshoff in 1896. In racing the fin-keel type is still very popular.

At the end of *Gloriana's* first season, Herreshoff got another order for a 46-footer and the result was *Wasp*, launched the following spring. *Wasp* was like the *Gloriana* in most details but she was even larger (except on the waterline, of course) and even more powerful, a refinement of *Gloriana*. *Wasp's* superiority was so complete that over the next several years she nearly killed interest in the class.

Edward Burgess died the summer that *Gloriana* went on the water, and when the next America's Cup challenge was issued, for the summer of 1893, Herreshoff got two orders for candidates to defend. Of the two, the one chosen for the international race was *Vigilant*, the first yacht whose bottom was plated with Tobin bronze, a metal with a smoother surface than the steel of the time. *Vigilant*, like her challenger, was 85 feet on the waterline (the dimension was a condition of the challenge). Her heavily weighted keel ran 14 feet (the maximum depth of water off the Herreshoff plant), and below this there swung a centerboard. *Vigilant* beat her challenger, *Valkyrie II*, in three straight races, beginning Herreshoff's string of six consecutive victories in the America's Cup. Only one of Herreshoff's Cup defenders ever lost a race in Cup competition. She was *Resolute*, of the 1920 series. She lost the first two races that year, but came back to take the series of five.

Herreshoff's brother, John, who had been the business head of the firm since it began, died in 1915. Nathanael, who was the designer, engineer, and experimenter, but not a businessman, gradually lost control of the corporation, and he retired as the business passed into other hands in 1924. Without Herreshoff and his brother, the company did not operate well, and it was liquidated shortly after World War II. Herreshoff himself died at his home in Bristol in 1938.

Herreshoff was a unique person, a contemporary of Henry Ford and the Wright brothers, who was born at the right time and had the vision to make the most of it in the dawn of modern technology. His time also was one in which there was demand for very expensive yachts. *Defender*, his America's Cup boat of 1895, had steel frames, a bottom of manganese bronze, and topsides of aluminum, which in those days was slightly less valuable than gold. Use of the aluminum lowered *Defender's* center of gravity, to be sure, but, like the rest of the big yachts of the time, she was incredibly expensive. But the time was one generation after the exciting rivalries of the clipper ships, and one generation before automobiles and airplanes, a time when the wealthy had little else on which to spend their money, and few means to go anywhere on Saturdays and Sundays, except down to the yacht club.

Herreshoff himself was a mixture of artist and scientist. He designed a boat by carving a model of the hull, whittling and sanding it until the form felt and looked right to him. When done, he would place the model (actually they were half models) into the bed of an instrument he had had made for the purpose and measure the distances up, out, and over from some reference point, usually the lowest point of the keel. All these measurements, from several dozen or several hundred points on the model, were systematically recorded in a notebook. The measurements were scaled up to full size, then taken out to the shop, and lofted full size in the mold loft. Except for construction details, no drawings were involved.

The riggings on Herreshoff boats were no enduring triumph. With his ability as an engineer, Herreshoff figured out ways to put up huge amounts of canvas and keep it there, but there are rigs in existence today that would drive a Herreshoff boat just as fast while using little more than half the sail area that Herreshoff himself used. Such modern, efficient rigs were a spinoff from the science of aerodynamics, which came with the airplane.

Herreshoff's hull configurations have been the most enduring aspect of his work. His methods of hull construction, while very advanced in their time, have long since been superseded, but the shapes of the hulls have not.

IV Small Boats and New Ideas

In spite of the tremendous numbers of them today, the sailing of small boats, either for racing or just for fun, was practically unheard of before 1900.

There were a couple of exceptions, one being the "sandbaggers" of the area around New York City, Long Island Sound, and the Jersey coast. The sandbaggers were cheap, dish-shaped machines that were raced with cutthroat enthusiasm on Sunday afternoons. Aboard them rode a crew of ten or twelve men and a ton or two of sand, sewn up in 50-pound or 100-pound bags. The boats carried so much rigging that they literally would not stand up if left unattended at a buoy. The sand was ballast, and the bags were all thrown over against the weather rail when the boat was under way. When the boat changed tack, the crewmen worked feverishly shifting the ballast (and themselves) over to the other rail.

Shifting the ballast, of course, made the boats sail more nearly upright, which increased power in the sails and therefore increased speed. In technical terms, the center of gravity was being moved away from the center of buoyancy. The distance between the two centers was being increased, which increased the leverage of the righting arm.

We made quite a point in a previous chapter that the center of gravity of a boat never shifts, but the case of the sandbaggers is, in a sense, an exception. Any time weight within a boat is shifted, its center of gravity shifts.

Another exception is the Chesapeake Bay log canoe, a fast design that originated in the 1870's or 1880's. A modern version is still sailed today.

The log canoes are small vessels with long, thin hulls and powerful rigs. Elaborate measures are taken to use human bodies as shifting ballast. Today, as in the 1880's, two long planks are carried aboard. When the boat is under way, the ends of the planks are hooked beneath the lee rail and from there the planks run athwartship, across the weather rail, and out over the water. Two members of the crew (there are three altogether) then get out on the boards, and their weight becomes outboard ballast. Like the sandbags, the bodies of these "hiking boards," as they are called, shift the center of gravity to the weather side.

Shifting ballast, be it human weight or some other kind of weight, is something that works out well on small boats. It is very common in racing dinghys today to see people hanging over the weather side, their ankles hooked into straps and the crooks of their knees over the weather rail.

Few sailors today use hiking boards, and we know of no boats that carry sandbags any more. In the last few years, however, trapezes have come into common use in many racing classes. A trapeze is a wire, one end secured up on the mast, the other end fitted with a harness. A crewman hangs overboard, swinging from the harness as he balances himself with his feet on the rail.

The gymnastics of hanging over a rail or of throwing sandbags around are generally for racing enthusiasts only. Shifting ballast, human or otherwise, is either impractical or of little affect on big boats. The Americans did pull a fast one in the America's Cup race of 1895 by putting seventy of the huskiest men they could find aboard *Defender*. Only about a dozen of them were needed to operate the boat, so the job of the rest was simple: to stand up against the weather rail and when the boat changed tack, walk across the deck to the other rail. After this race, the rules were changed to prevent this practice.

But for casual sailing in small boats, the shift is usually confined to the practice of having everyone aboard sit on the seats on the weather side. Anything beyond this is unpleasantly tiresome on a long-range basis.

A hull design evolved in the 1880's and 1890's that works well on small boats, but is generally a failure on big boats. The failure is not the fault

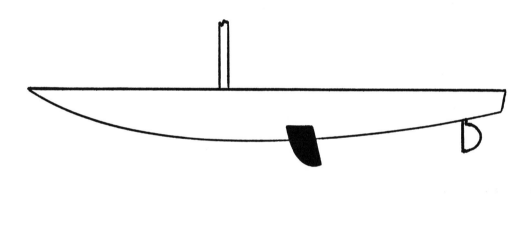

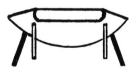

SCOW. The scow is a type of hull that evolved, in varying detail, around the turn of the century. It is characterized by a broad beam and very shallow draft. The hull is meant to sail heeled over to one side and then to the other, and to this end the modern versions have two rudders and two bilgeboards (which are the same thing as centerboards except that they are on the bilges instead of in the center). When under way, scows raise themselves up in the water and skim along the surface at high speed— as long as the water is smooth. Scows perform very poorly, and are very uncomfortable, in a chop or high waves. The hull type is fine for high speed, but good for little else.

of the bigness; it is just that the hull design is not much good except on the relatively calm waters of small lakes. The design is the scow, and the best way to describe it is to say that it is two hulls in one. However, a scow is *not* a catamaran—catamarans are vessels with two separate hulls.

Scow hulls are the shape of an elongated saucer, and as they eventually evolved, they have two centerboards (or bilge boards, as they are called) and two rudders. When the hull is sitting quietly at anchor, both sets of bilge boards and rudders will be in the water, even though they are on opposite sides of the hull and are toed away from each other.

When the boat is under way, the hull will be heeled at about a 20-degree angle. The boat is designed to rock over to that angle and become stable there. At this angle of heel the bilge board and the rudder on the weather side will be out of the water (or nearly so), even if they are in the down position. The bilge board and rudder on the lee side will be directly under the portion of the hull that is in the water, and the lee bilge board and rudder will then be vertical.

Scows—the successful ones, at least—are of very light construction. Their motion through the water tends to cause the hull to lift itself toward the surface, allowing it to skim along, or plane, as it has come to be called. Because of the positions of the rudder and bilge board, the scows are quite controllable in spite of the skimming.

The scow was not an invention that happened all at once at a certain time in a certain place. The design just evolved over several years. The sandbaggers, though they did not have the double rudder and bilge board, were scow-type hulls. Herreshoff's *Dilemma* also was a scow-type hull ballasted with a fin keel. *Dilemma* also had a single rudder.

Scows are completely worthless for anything except racing, and they are even worthless for racing on anything except inland lakes or water that otherwise is well sheltered. They haven't the slightest room for accommodations, and the smaller ones don't even have room for seats. In a sea they would be wet and slow part of the time and upside down the rest of the time. But on smooth water, scows are very fast, even in just a breath of air.

There are four one-design classes of scows today that are very popular throughout the upper Midwest and in Ontario. Large fleets of one class or the other can be found on many inland lakes throughout Wisconsin, Minnesota, and Michigan. The four classes are A (38-foot length overall), E (28-foot), C (20-foot), and M (16-foot).

Wisconsin has for fifty years been the center of scow racing, and numerous refinements in the type have come from the one-design classes that race there. Nearly all the one-design scows are built there.

In the United States, interest in small sailboats started booming just after the turn of the century. Racing among fleets of small boats, and cruising and day-sailing in small boats, began spreading across the country and growing every year except in wartime and, perhaps, during the Depression.

Ever since the boom started, development and the search for speed has gone over, more and more, to small boats. Before World War I, most development was in big boats and little boats picked up pointers from their larger cousins. Before many years just the opposite was true.

One of the first things that made its debut on small boats but was later adopted by big boats was the Marconi sail. It appeared in about 1910. The Marconi is the familiar fore-and-aft triangular. It is the mainsail on about 95 percent of sailboats today.

At the time the Marconi rig was invented, the gaff-rig was practically the universal sail on small boats, but over the years the gaff had become shorter and shorter. Perhaps it became so short that someone just eliminated it and ran the leech (the after edge of the canvas) all the way to the mast. For years before 1910, big boats all carried topsails above the gaff that filled out the triangle. The mainsail and the topsail together were a triangle anyway. All that remained to make the rig a Marconi was to connect the mainsail and topsail into a continuous piece of canvas and throw away the stick between them.

The Marconi rig has several advantages over the gaff rig. Elimination of the gaff reduces weight aloft; the shape is more naturally aerodynamic, because it has less tendency to bag and twist; and the rig is handier because there is only sailcloth, no stick of wood, to haul aloft.

The gaff sail, being quadrilateral, does present more area to the wind for a given size mast and boom. To make up for this deficiency in area, Marconi rigs have always been generally higher (with respect to hull size) than gaff rigs, and it is partly because of this height that the rig picked up the name "Marconi." At about the same time the rig appeared, Guglielmo Marconi, the Italian who won a Nobel Prize for his work in wireless telegraphy, was promoting the wireless as a safety device for ships. Old-time sailors viewed both the wireless and the new sailing rigs with suspicion, and one of them dubbed the rig "Marconi" because the high mast resembled the antenna towers of the wireless stations.

The height was not the only resemblance, however. At about the same time as the Marconi sail, jumper stays, multiple stays, and multiple shrouds all came into vogue, and on most boats even back then, the stays and shrouds were of wire rope. Wire rope was first manufactured by machine beginning about 1850, and it was so superior to fiber rope for standing rigging that it quickly was adopted.

On masts rigged with fore-and-aft sails, standing rigging (shrouds, stays, etc.) ran from the top of the mast only until the invention of sail

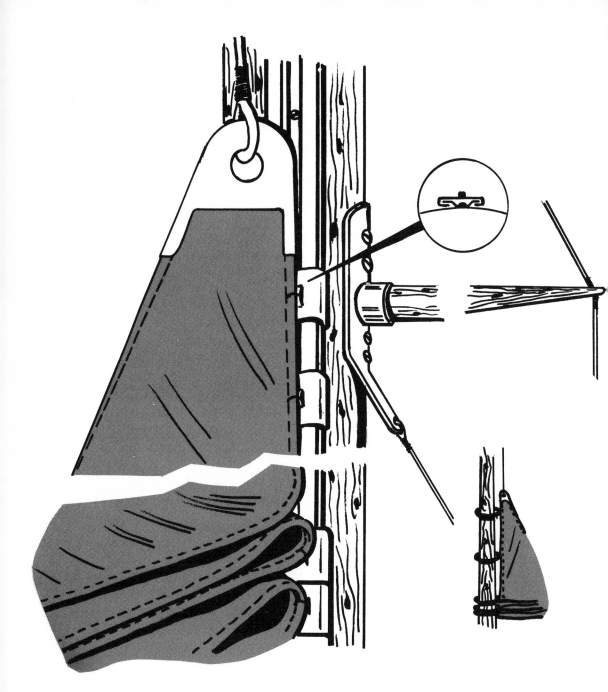

SAIL TRACK. Invented in the 1890's by Nathanael Herreshoff, sail track has been the key to the development of modern, high-power rigging. The sail is sewn to metal slides that hook over a metal rail, which is fastened along the mast. The track and slides not only provide a tight seal between the edge of the sail and the mast, but also allow the attachment of shrouds and spreaders at intermediate points on the mast. With the older arrangement of attaching the sail by hoops, which completely encircled the mast (shown at the lower right), no stays or shrouds could be attached to the mast except at the top, because they would have been in the way of the hoops, which had to slide up and down the mast. To slide freely, the hoops had to be loose-fitting, and this resulted in a poor seal between the sail and the mast.

track. Before sail track the sails were fastened with hoops that completely encircled the mast. In order for the hoops to slide up and down as the sail was raised and lowered, it was not possible to attach anything to the mast below the point to which the highest hoop was to run.

Herreshoff invented sail track in about 1890, and it had come into common use by 1910. The track consists of a strip of metal, usually brass, about an inch wide, that runs vertically on the after side of the mast and is fastened there by screws. Each edge of the strip is raised into a flange. Metallic slides slip onto these flanges, and though the slides are free to run along the strip (or track), they cannot come off, except at the lower end.

The slides have eyes, and through them the slides are sewn all along the luff (the leading edge) of the sail. Hoops are eliminated. Raising a sail is simply a matter of feeding the slides onto the track with one hand and pulling the halyard with the other. Track and slides also are used to fasten the foot of the sail along the boom.

Sail track is much more convenient than hoops, it makes a closer seal between the mast and the sailcloth (which is an aerodynamic advantage), it can be fitted to a mast of a better aerodynamic shape (hoops work well only on a tubular shape), and it permits the attachment of intermediate stays and shrouds to the sides and the front of the mast, because they no longer form an impediment to raising and lowering the sail.

Designers and builders were not long in taking advantage of the benefits of sail track. By attaching stays and shrouds at several points and running them over spreaders, masts were stiffened by external bracing. The masts then required less internal stiffness, with the result that they could be made lighter and weight aloft was saved.

Spreaders are crossarms on the mast. If a mast is equipped with a spreader, then the shrouds, anchored by heavy strapping through the planking at deck level down to the keel, travel upward and bend over the ends of the spreaders before passing on above to the point at which they are fastened to the mast. With a spreader, the tension in the shrouds is distributed to two points on the mast, one point being where the shroud itself is anchored to the mast, the other point being where the spreader is attached to the mast. With the load distributed, the mast is less likely to buckle and so can be made lighter.

Jumper staying, another device for distributing load and stiffening externally, also involves a crossarm on the mast. However, the wire ropes that pass over the crossarm (jumper strut) do not go to the deck. The ends are both fastened to the mast, one end being above the strut, the other below. If the strut runs athwartship, then the jumper stays are always in pairs (one over each end of the strut) and they form the shape of a dia-

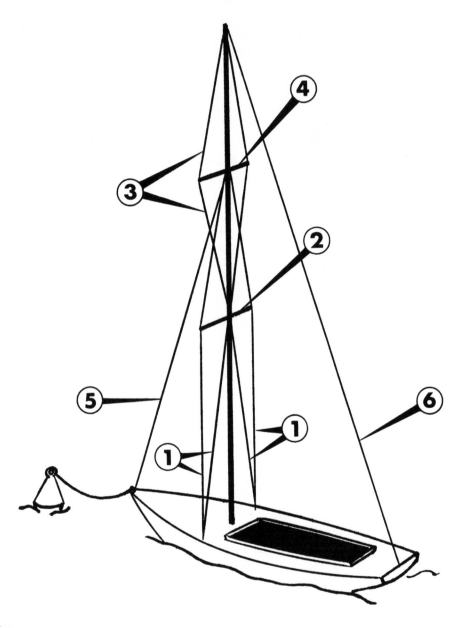

STANDING RIGGING. The use of sail track has made it possible to attach external bracing at intermediate points along the mast, where before, when hoops were used to attach the sail, it was possible to brace the mast only from the top. The parts of the external bracing now commonly used are: (1) shrouds, (2) spreader, (3) jumper stays, (4) jumper strut, (5) forestay. The use of a Marconi sail has made it possible to attach a standing backstay (6) from the peak of the mast. The Marconi sail, which is cut in a triangle, swings freely inside the backstay, whereas the backstay would have been in the way of the gaff on the older type of sail.

mond—consequently they are sometimes called diamonds. Some masts have "half-diamonds," which run fore-and-aft on the forward side.

The diamonds and half-diamonds increased the resemblance of masts to wireless antennas.

None of this multiple staying was possible until sail track came into use, and none of it would have worked very well if fiber rope was all that was available. Fiber rope shrinks and stretches and complex systems of staying would constantly go out of adjustment. One could not have whittled a mast very thin with any confidence that such a rig would hold it. Wire rope, on the other hand, is susceptible to only minute changes in dimension and is very reliable for external bracing.

The load on any mast, unless the stays and shrouds let go, is straight down. If you figured that your sail generated 5,000 pounds of energy, then the entire stress on your mast would be the same as if there were a 5,000-pound weight strapped along it. All of the lateral energy is carried in the stays and shrouds, which convert the force to thrust downward in the mast. For this reason, masts are built to have great strength in compression, but to save weight, they are cut thin and can stand very little side load.

If you placed a mast from a small boat across two saw horses and then jumped up and down on it in the middle, you would have little trouble breaking it with nothing more than your own weight. But if you stood the same mast on its end and stayed it well enough so that it couldn't buckle, it could easily withstand the weight of a small automobile.

Most mast failures are preceded by buckling. Occasionally masts shatter from compression alone, but for the most part a stay or shroud either snaps or is out of adjustment when a mast breaks. Even a slight buckle diverts a portion of the stresses from compression to sidethrust, and the diversion increases rapidly as the buckle increases.

The masts of most family cruising boats have a generous margin of strength, both internally and in the gauge of the wire rope staying them externally. The masts of racing sailboats, on the other hand, are usually shaved to the last ounce. The wire rope staying them is as thin as possible, to reduce both weight and wind resistance, and the rigs are subject to a high rate of failure.

Hollow masts, of either wood or metal, have greater resistance to buckling than solid masts of the same amount of material. In other words, their strength-to-weight ratio is higher. The reason is that the two walls work with each other, one in tension, the other in compression, to resist side load. In the solid masts, or in spars in general, the material in the center is of no value in resisting buckling, because it neither takes compression or tension. In fact, material in the center may actually weaken a solid spar, because in a buckle, the center material is pressed upon by the compressed

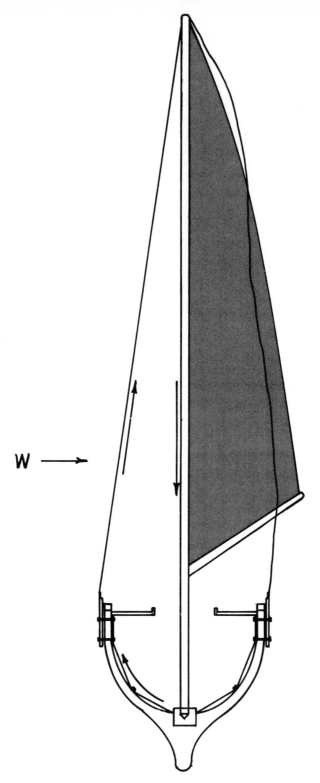

W ⟶

MAST LOAD. All of the stress on a properly stayed mast is compression. The pressure on the mast, which is actually to the side as the wind blows onto the sail, is converted to downward energy by the stays or shrouds that are to windward. Equal to the force of compression in the mast is an opposite force of tension in the stays. Thus if the force in compression in the mast is 5,000 pounds, the tension on the stays is 5,000 pounds. Only the stays to windward are ever in use on a rig. The stays to lee are slack.

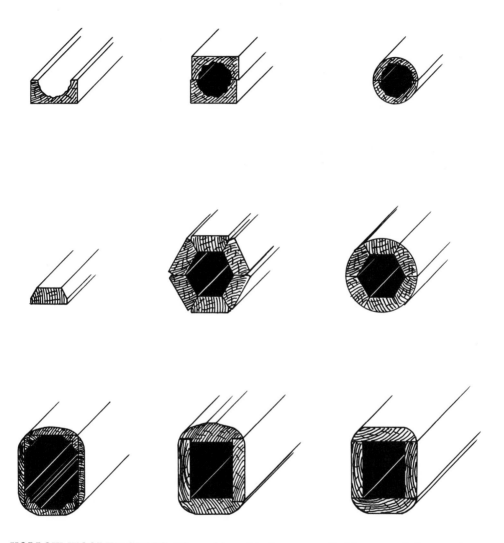

HOLLOW WOODEN SPARS. The making of hollow spars, first booms and then masts, began in the early 1800's. The purpose of hollowing, particularly in the case of masts, is to save weight aloft. Nearly all modern masts, whether they are wood or metal, are hollow. The earliest hollow spars were constructed of two boards that had a hand-routed trough for their entire length (upper left). The two boards were then glued up, trough to trough (upper center), and then turned round (upper right). The method was crude and wall thicknesses often were not uniform. In the late 1800's, Nathanael Herreshoff glued up hollow spars out of six staves and then turned them round (three center drawings, left to right). Though aluminum is now becoming very popular as a material for spars, many wooden spars are still used today, and most are of the box type. The bottom row of drawings shows three different methods of fabricating box spars. The most simple construction is the one at the right.

side, and it in turn presses out on the tension side, becoming in effect a fulcrum over which the tension side can crack.

Hollow spars did not come into common use until about 1900. The method of building them then was to rout hollows in two thick boards and then glue the boards together with the hollows facing each other. After the glue dried, the mast was rounded into a tubular shape. Masts built up in this way often turned out poorly, because with hand tools it was very difficult to keep the walls uniformly thick.

Herreshoff developed a system of building up hollow wooden masts from six boards by beveling the edges, gluing them together into a long, six-sided box, and then rounding it into a tubular shape. These masts were very light and uniformly strong throughout, but were very tedious to build. Masts on most of Herreshoff's big boats were tubular steel.

The four-sided box spar, because it is much easier to build and nearly as strong as its weight, eventually became very popular, especially among amateur builders. Such spars are made of four boards, which can easily be clamped together for gluing. It is also an easy matter to taper the boards, thereby getting a tapered spar. The flat sides make it easy to mount sail track, spreaders, and attachments for stays.

The trouble with box spars is that they have a very poor aerodynamic shape. On either a Marconi or a gaff sail, the mast is the leading edge of what is actually an airfoil. Ideally, the mast and sail together should form a shape similar to that of the top of an airplane wing. Otherwise air will not flow smoothly and power will be lost.

When sailors became conscious of the problems of air flow, racing boats went for streamlined masts. A cross section of such a mast is teardrop-shaped, the sail being attached along the thin edge, and the rounded edge being the leading edge.

Streamlined masts can be hollow. When they are made of wood, they are built of two pieces that are routed and then glued together, just like the first tubular masts, but the exterior is then planed into the teardrop shape instead of being turned round. Modern power woodworking tools make construction much easier than it was at the turn of the century. Modern tools also make control of dimensions much easier.

Many masts today are extruded of aluminum. Nearly all are of streamlined shape.

V Design by the Rules

Since the end of commercial sailing, racing sailboats have been the primary vehicles of development, and boat design has been greatly affected by the requirements of difficult types of racing. The most obvious differences are between boats designed for long-distance racing and those designed for short distances.

Long races, as across an ocean, require that boats be large and strong because they must be able to withstand high winds and heavy seas, they must be able to carry enough men for separate watches, they must have quarters large enough to accommodate this crew, they must have room enough for stores for several men for several days or weeks, depending on the length of the race, and they must carry navigational equipment and survival gear.

Short-distance racing boats, such as those around a set of marks on a Sunday afternoon, need none of these provisions, except that everyone should have a life jacket. Anyone who shows up for a Sunday-afternoon race with a heavily built and fully fitted ocean racer is going to be badly beaten by any short-distance boats of comparable size.

The scow, discussed in the previous chapter, is an example of a craft that is extremely fast on sheltered waters, but could never be adapted to race long distances out to sea. The scow has no room for stores or quarters, but more important, its hull, which skims along well in smooth water, has little freeboard and would swamp in even moderate seas. But on inland lakes or sheltered coastal waters, where harbors of refuge and rescue boats are never far away, the scow is a very fine and very fast vessel.

The differences between an ocean racer and a scow are an extreme—though real—example of the ways boats differ according to the conditions in which they are to be raced. There are other ways that are more subtle.

Sunday-afternoon races, for instance, are usually several laps around a set of marks (buoys) placed in a triangle with sides 1 to 3 miles long. Around such a course a boat will first have to sail against the wind (beat), then sail with the wind at its side (reach), and finally sail with the wind at its stern (run). The sails and the rigging must be efficient on all of these different points of sailing.

Furthermore, the turns in between the different legs are critical maneuvers. The boats have to be designed so that they have a short turning radius, and the tackle and hardware must be laid out so that sails may be reset in a matter of seconds.

On the other hand, most ocean races are in straight lines. Changing and resetting sails are infrequent tasks, and the tackle and gear for handling sails need not be so sophisticated. Tight turns are seldom necessary, and in fact a boat that responds quickly to turning is generally undesirable in ocean racing, because such boats require much closer attention to keep them on a straight course.

Though it seldom happens any more, it is possible to design a boat for one specific ocean race. There are cases of boats being built for the Bermuda Race, for instance, where the winds are predominantly at a right angle to the course. Boats built especially for this race can be rigged to make sails more efficient in beam winds, even to the detriment of efficiency in beating or running. The boat also can be ballasted somewhat lighter, since it is not expected to have to beat, the point of sailing on which stability gets the stiffest challenge.

Winds and waves and the necessity to maneuver are not the only things that influence boat design, however. One must take account of the fact that big boats are naturally faster than small boats. To have races it is necessary to equalize the potential performance of the boats entered. There are four basic systems for doing this: measurement for time allowance, measurement for classification, development class rules, and one-design class rules.

Measurement goes back well into the 1800's, if not farther. In the beginning it was very simple—something like giving a smaller boat a head start of a certain number of minutes or hours in proportion to the length of its hull at the waterline.

The rules for measuring, called rating rules, may have worked well at first because they were written and applied to boats that were already in existence. Trouble began after the rule was written because competitors could have a boat designed and built in such a way as to take advantage of the rule and get a big time allowance, for example by putting an unusually large (and dangerous) amount of sail on a small hull. The rule then had to be rewritten and the formula lengthened to include a penalty for sail area that was disproportionately large for the waterline length.

Rating rules, as they have changed (usually by becoming more complicated), are written to favor "safe, wholesome, all-around boats," a nice ideal, but one with some pitfalls. In the first place, owners of existing boats tend to protect their investments by writing rules that penalize genuine development. Rules-committee meetings become political platforms that retard development by keeping it channeled along strict, conventional lines. And in spite of such conservatism, it has not been possible to write rules so tightly that there are no loopholes. Designers find loopholes and exploit them. But because of the restrictions surrounding the loophole, the design that exploits it often turns out to be an unsafe, though fast freak rather than a "wholesome, all-around boat."

Two of the more famous loophole exploiters were Herreshoff's *Gloriana* and *Dilemma*. *Gloriana*, though she was a radical departure from existing practice, cannot properly be called a freak. Her basic gimmick was long, overhanging ends to provide reserve buoyancy, a large platform for large rigging, and added length at the waterline when heeled. Time has proved all of these innovations to be legitimate progress. *Dilemma*, on the other hand, was a freak. Being closely related to the scow, she was of very limited usefulness even though under certain conditions of wind and sea she was very fast.

The whole history of rating rules is the appearance of successive freaks and the rewriting of the formulas to plug the loopholes. Some of the rating rules have gotten longer and longer until today naval architects must also be lawyers, and it takes a day and many expensive instruments to measure a boat for rating and another day to work out the formula.

There are dozens or even hundreds of rating rules, many of them local, others regional, and a few national or international. The present trend is for local and regional rules to be abolished and national rules to be adopted instead for local and regional regattas.

Long-distance ocean races, such as the Trans Pac, the Bermuda, and the Mackinac, are all run under rating rules. The Mackinac Races, run on the

Great Lakes, are not, strictly speaking, ocean races, but they attract the same type of racers—big, expensive boats that are built and fitted out to highly individual tastes for long voyages. Rating is the only practical way to handicap boats of such widely differing characteristics.

Rating rules yield numbers that, theoretically, are ratios of the speeds attainable by the boats so rated. Even if the ratios were perfect, the problem still remains of how to convert them to time.

The practice in American yachting is to take the differential in the ratios, multiply the ratio by a fixed number of minutes and seconds, and then multiply that product by the number of miles in the race. It is called the "time on distance" method.

The British generally apply their ratings as a factor of actual elapsed time. In other words, the corrected time is a percentage of actual time, the percentages being in proportion to the ratings. This is called the "time on time" method.

Beginning in 1972, the International Offshore Rule has begun a procedure that will abolish time allowance under IOR by 1975. Boats are still to be rated, but instead of giving time allowances, the boats will be put into nineteen different classes. Boats in the different classes will race each other without time allowance. The only difficulty may be that classes in some races will have only one boat, but the number of sailboats in the world is increasing rapidly, so this may not be a problem.

There is no time allowance in either development classes or one-design classes. The first boat across the finsh line wins (unless a foul has been committed.)

Development classes began in the late 1800's. Their rules are a loose set of limits on waterline length, overall length, sail area, etc. Some development-class rules are very simple, such as specifying maximum overall length only or maximum sail area only. Others are much more complicated and specify ratios of ballast weight to overall weight, ballast weight to sail area, or length to sail area.

There have not been many genuine innovations to come out of development classes. The effect of the rules has been to force designers to concentrate on details of hull configuration, rudder placement, rudder shape, centerboard shape, weight-saving construction, and a myriad of other minor considerations, which add up to a lot of speed when all taken together.

Innovations from the development classes have been picked up and incorporated into many one-design boats. Small catamarans, started through the development-class phase in the 1960's, and one-design classes of catamarans, based on what had been learned in development racing, are beginning to emerge.

The older development-class rules and those with more complicated formulas have come to some of the same grief as rating rules. The rules have become so restrictive that in effect they are statutes to preserve the status quo, rather than to encourage development. The most famous development-class event, the America's Cup, is an example. Twelve-meter yachts, which have done all of the racing for the Cup since World War II, are built to complicated restrictions set down in 1904 and 1905. Innovations such as masthead jibs and spade runners, both of which have long since proved out and are commonly used on many boats, are prohibited in the class.

There is a fine line between the more restrictive development classes and the more liberal one-design classes. Theoretically, one-design classes are composed of a fleet of boats that are identical. Racing them is supposed to be a contest of ability to sail, since all boats are presumed to be equal.

There were local one-design classes in the 1890's. The first class that became regional, the *Star*, was formed at New York in 1911. A *Star* is a 22-foot keelboat that was originally a gaff-rigged sloop, but the rules have since been changed over to Marconi rigging. Today there are *Star* fleets all over the world.

The largest class today in number of boats is the *Snipe*, a 15-foot daggerboard sloop. (A daggerboard functions exactly like a centerboard, but the mechanics are different: while a centerboard swings up and down on a pin, a daggerboard is not pinned but is just a straight piece of board, lowered and pulled up by hand.) There are approximately 15,000 *Snipes* in the water.

The theory that all boats of the same design are identical has not worked out in practice. This has been a very good thing for development in sailboats, though it has been bad for some of the classes.

Most one-design specifications succeed in rigidly controlling the shape of the hull, the dimensions of the spars, and the sail area. What they do not control is the cut of sails, the sail-handling hardware, and the deck layout of the hardware and the lines. The result has been many happy improvements. Since the one-design skippers have not been permitted to experiment with anything else, they have been forced to concentrate their attention on getting more power out of their sails and on finding ways to handle sails faster when rounding marks.

Development classes and iceboats were the forerunners in improving the general shape of rigging, but the one-designers, along with iceboaters, have done most of the work in applying aerodynamic principles to sails. One-designs have been an excellent laboratory for this kind of improvement, because a new sail or a new method of tuning the rigging can be tested against boats that in all other respects are identical.

The unhappy aspect of these developments has been that some boats have become very costly. One-design classes, as they were originally conceived, were to provide inexpensive, yet competitive racing. Many of the classes have gone through so much sophistication that boats become outmoded when they are only a few years old. Keeping up with developments, either by buying a new boat or refitting an old one, has become too expensive for many sailors, and so of necessity they drop out of the class.

Today there are hundreds of one-design classes with fleets of boats in yacht clubs all over the nation, or even over the world. Most one-design boats can be transported on trailers behind cars, and many of the more popular classes have national regattas.

VI Iceboat Design

Many of the refinements in sails and rigging that have been developed since World War I originated on iceboats.

Iceboaters, mostly those in the area of Wisconsin, were the first to make good use of aerodynamics, a branch of knowledge that was a spinoff from the aircraft industry. Airplanes rapidly became sophisticated during that first war, and in the twenty years that followed, iceboats also became very sophisticated.

Many of the developments in iceboats in that era have gradually come over to "soft-water" boats, and they are very useful to racing yachtsmen as well as to yachtsmen who simply cruise or go day-sailing.

To sum up these developments in one phrase, one could say that sails are much, much more efficient. They are more powerful for their size. A modern sail can now drive a hull just as fast as the old-style sail of nearly twice the area.

Iceboaters in general have always been an uninhibited lot. With little exception, their machines have never been instruments of commerce. Iceboats are things of sport, and experimenters have not had to buck the hard-nosed tradition that designers have encountered in the conservative soft-water field.

Iceboats were probably the first things on earth purposely to carry human beings faster than 100 miles per hour. By a wide margin, they are the fastest machines in existence that are not powered mechanically or by gravity. Until the past few years, when a few soft-water boats and land yachts followed suit, iceboats were the only sailing machines that could actually sail faster than the speed of the wind that propelled them.

One of the reasons iceboat development has been so rapid is that iceboat design has not been impeded by the safety considerations that are necessary to the design of soft-water boats. There are seldom drownings in iceboating, and what drownings there are result from a condition in the ice plus carelessness, not because of any defect in the boat.

In spite of their high speeds, iceboats are rather safe vehicles. Even if an iceboat disintegrates or flips over, putting bodies into thin air at 100 miles per hour, the bodies will be moving nearly parallel to a smooth, unabrasive surface. Though the bodies may slide a long way and lose some of their skin, they nearly always survice. Few are even hurt much. The biggest danger in iceboating is that of hitting an obstruction, such as an ice-fishing shanty, or colliding with another iceboat. Most of the serious injuries occur in one of these two fashions.

Iceboats, or ice yachts as they also are called, apparently originated in the Netherlands in the eighteenth century. It is there that we find the only long-lasting and serious use of iceboats in commerce.

The small soft-water boats in the Netherlands had broad, flat bottoms with leeboards for lateral resistance. For the winter, when the canals and lakes were frozen, some of the Dutch seamen would convert these boats for use on ice by taking off the leeboards and fastening three large, skate-like runners to the hull. Two of the runners were at opposite ends of a stout plank that was bolted crosswise beneath the hull directly below the mast. The other runner was on the bottom of a special rudder that supported the hull at the stern.

An engraving dated 1768 shows a flat-bottomed sloop fitted out in this manner. The sails are the usual for that time and place—gaff main and forestaysail—and it seems certain that the same rig was used in both winter and summer. We know nothing of the boat's speed or of the speed of iceboats in general of that era, but it is likely that the boat depicted in the engraving could outsail the summer version of itself. It could not have been really fast, though, because of its weight.

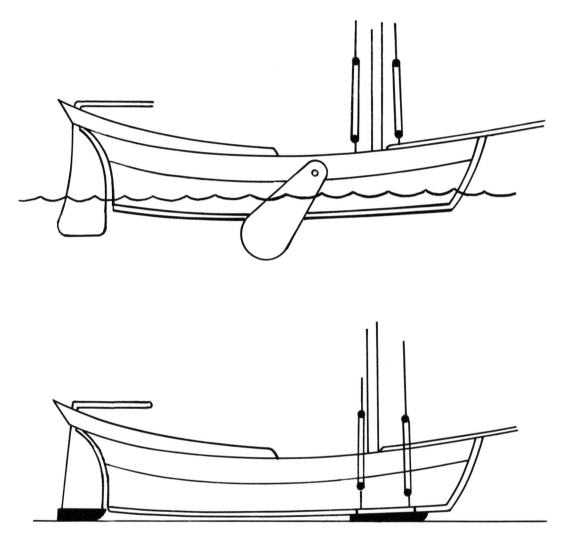

WINTER-SUMMER BOAT. Because they operate in shallow canals, small Dutch sailing boats have always been of the flat-bottom type with leeboards for lateral resistance when out to sea. The earliest iceboats were apparently conversions of these soft-water boats. The canals in the Netherlands freeze over in the winter, so the Dutch jacked up their vessels and set their flat bottoms on a plank that ran crosswise, more or less beneath the mast step. At each end of the plank was a skatelike runner. At the stern, the summer rudder was replaced with a shortened rudder that had a runner on its bottom. So equipped, the Dutch sailed on their canals in winter as well as summer, beginning in the 1700's.

As far as we know, the first iceboat on this side of the Atlantic was built at Poughkeepsie, New York, by Oliver Booth in 1790. It had two runners in front, one at either end of a plank, and a single runner at the stern. The body was an oblong box that may have been the bed from a horse-drawn wagon. From the stern runner, a rudder post ran up the back of the box, and from the top of this post, the tiller came inboard.

The rig was a single, rather low fore-and-aft spritsail, and the sailcloth was probably linen, the universal material for ship sails at the time. The mast stood at the front of the box, with the leading edge of the sail lashed by a continuous line that spiraled around and around the mast, passing through cloth on each turn.

Through the early 1800's, interest in iceboating increased, and the Hudson River was the center of activity. By 1850 or 1860 the prevailing design had changed to that of single, T-shaped frame. The T consisted of the traverse runner plank in front and a single, longitudinal member that ran aft from the runner plank to the stern runner, which was still the steering runner.

The box bed had been pretty much eliminated in favor of a small platform, enclosed only by rails, near the stern. There were three reasons for this. First, by 1850, the search for speed was on and the box was an obvious source of wind resistance. Second, iceboats were getting bigger, and a platform the full length of the frame was no longer necessary to accommodate the crew. Finally, weight was needed at the back to improve control.

The biggest problem with these early iceboats was that they had a lot of weather helm. The center of lateral resistance on stern-steering ice boats is the forward lee runner. With the mast stepped right over the runner plank, the center of effort of the sail is considerably aft of the CLR, and the result is that the stern of the boat always wants to swing to lee, allowing the boat to head up. This problem was not serious in older, slower boats, but as speeds were increased, vibration and bouncing increased also, and this caused the stern runner to lose its track more easily. The more speed increased, the more likely the runner was to lose its grip. Moving the crew to the stern helped the problem and added several miles per hour to the boats, but control remained the limiting problem in the search for speed.

The fore-and-aft spritsail lost popularity (if it ever had any) with ice-boaters, and most Hudson River boats had a gaff-rigged mainsail plus a jib by the time of the Civil War.

Iceboats, like soft-water yachts, went through a phase of bigness, with big money behind them and professional crews running them. The era was similar to that of the Herreshoff era in soft water, but in iceboating this so-called "golden age" came fifteen or twenty years earlier.

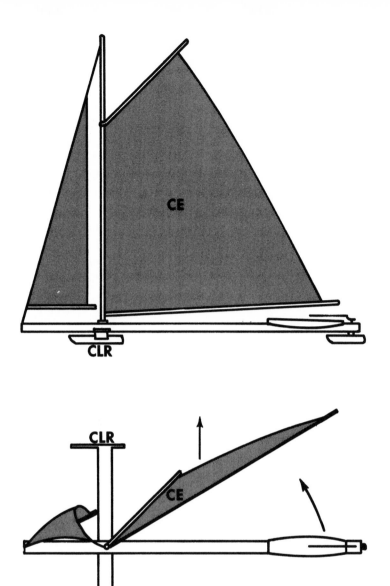

EARLY SPORT ICEBOATS. In the mid-1800's, iceboating became a popular sport on the Hudson River in New York State. Many iceboats of 40 to 70 feet in length were built with T-shaped frames, which had two stationary runners set wide apart in front and a single runner turned by a tiller at the stern. These stern-steerers became known as the Hudson River type. The usual sail plan was sloop-rig, with a large gaff mainsail and a small jib. The mast was stepped directly over the runner plank, causing the fault that the center of effort of the sail plan was aft of the center of lateral resistance (the two front runners). The result was a pressure on the stern to go to lee (note arrows in bottom drawing). The fault was not serious in the early days of low speeds, but as speeds were increased over the years and the stern runner jiggled faster and faster over the ice, it became more and more difficult for the stern runner to hold its track.

The Poughkeepsie Ice Yacht Club, the first in the United States, was formed in 1865, and a few years later the Hudson River Ice Yacht Club was formed at Hyde Park with John E. Roosevelt, an uncle of F. D. R., as commodore. Other clubs were formed at New Hamburg and Chelsea.

Roosevelt was the owner of *Icicle*, which is probably the biggest iceboat ever built. *Icicle* was the creation of Jacob E. Buckhout, of Poughkeepsie. Jacob and his brother, George, became quite well known. They designetd and built many very expensive machines. They were to iceboating what Herreshoff was to soft-water yachts a few years later.

Icicle, built about 1870, was 70 feet long and carried over 1,000 square feet of sail. She was built of butternut wood cut from the Roosevelt estate at Hyde Park, and she was so big that she had to be transported to the ice on a railroad flatcar. For many years *Icicle* dominated the sport, winning the Ice Yacht Challenge Pennant of America (the America's Cup of ice yachting) time and again.

The problem of control at high speed was lessened in 1879 when a boat was built that had the mast sitting on the backbone a few feet *forward* of the runner plank instead of directly over it. The whole sail plan was moved forward. The combined center of effort was over the center of lateral resistance. This, of course, balanced the helm and made it less critical that the steering runner keep its grip.

This design was quickly copied and adapted to many more of the Hudson River types, and in a short time races were being run at speeds nearing 100 miles per hour. The boat that started this trend was the *Robert Scott*, built by a man named Relyea—his first name seems to have been lost over the years.

The moving of the mast forward was, however, a mixed blessing. The net effect was an increase in control, but with the mast forward of the runner plank, a new force was introduced that tended to lift the steering runner off of the ice. As was discussed in a previous chapter, the load on a mast is straight down, while there is an equal and opposite force up through the stays and/or shrouds. The mast was pushing down on the backbone at a point forward of the runner plank, so that the whole backbone in effect acted like a teeter-totter, with the runner plank being the fulcrum. With the front being pushed down, the stern would tend to come up, or at least it would tend to become lighter and take some of the grip off the steering runner. Since the shrouds ran aft from the mast to the runner plank, the upward force through them was completely neutral, with regard to this problem, and though the Hudson River boats were able to go much faster with the new design, lack of control still limited their potential speed.

At a very high speed, up near 100 miles per hour, nearly all of the weight of the boat is being carried on the lee runner. A sudden puff of wind or a

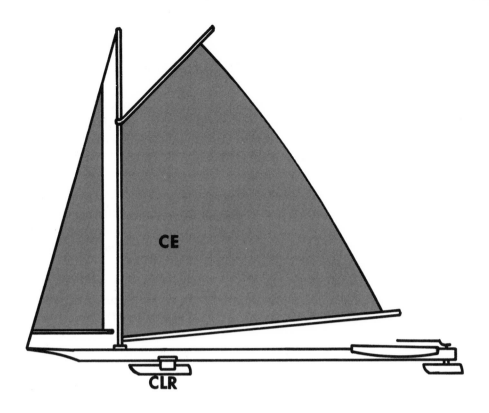

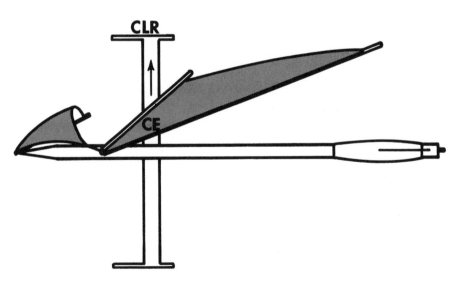

IMPROVEMENT IN CONTROL. Beginning in 1879, Hudson River type ice yachts were built with the mast stepped forward of the runner plank instead of on top of it. The design change brought the center of effort of the sail plan forward also so that it was horizontally aligned with the center of lateral resistance. The power of the sail no longer had leverage to force the stern to lee; the stern runner would stay on track and the machine could be kept under control at higher speed than those that had the mast stepped over the runner plank.

shift in the wind can cause an unexpected increase in power in the sails, and if the boat cannot accelerate fast enough to absorb this thrust, the boat will "hike" (the weather runner will raise up off the ice). Crews must be alert to control these hikes, either by heading up toward the wind or by slackening the sheets.

Stern steerers, whether they were of the old type with the mast over the runner plank or of the new type with mast forward, were most susceptible to going out of control during a hike. Loss of control usually resulted in a "flicker," the rather mild term used by iceboaters to mean a terrifying spin around the lee runner.

A new approach to rigging in the early 1880's helped lessen the control problem. Charles and William Merritt of Chelsea, New York, successfully adapted the lateen sail to an iceboat, and in a few years, their design had many imitators.

The design involved an A-frame for a mast with the legs stepped on the runner plank, one step on each side of the backbone. From the runner plank this A-frame leaned forward. The lateen sail, which had yards at both the top and the bottom, was hoisted between the legs of the A, and part of the sail stuck out in front of the mast.

The center of effort was over the runner plank, so that the helm was balanced, and since the sail pivoted on a point within the A-frame, the sail was partially counterbalanced, somewhat easing the work of the sheet tenders. In short, it was an easier rig to handle.

But in addition to this the problem of the mast bearing down on the backbone, causing the stern to lift, was eliminated. The downward thrust in the mast was neutralized because the steps of the A were on the runner plank, not on the backbone, and there was no more teeter-totter effect.

Lateen-riggers never became widely popular on the Hudson River. Iceboating there was severely curtailed, beginning in 1902, because in that year icebreakers began keeping the river open for navigation.

Large fleets of iceboats with lateen sails raced on the Navesink and Shrewsbury rivers in New Jersey in the early 1900's, and the type also was sailed in the Midwest. A timed run of 140 miles per hour is claimed for a lateen-rigger named *Clarel*, supposedly on the Shrewsbury River in 1908, but there are many who doubt this claim, both because accounts of the run contain mathematical errors and because it would be extremely difficult to keep any stern-steerer under control at such a speed.

The improvement in control brought by the lateen rig probably did push iceboating past 100 miles per hour. Lateen rigging, however, did not completely solve the control problem, for the stern-steerers would still flicker, though the tendency developed at a much higher speed than on sloop-riggers.

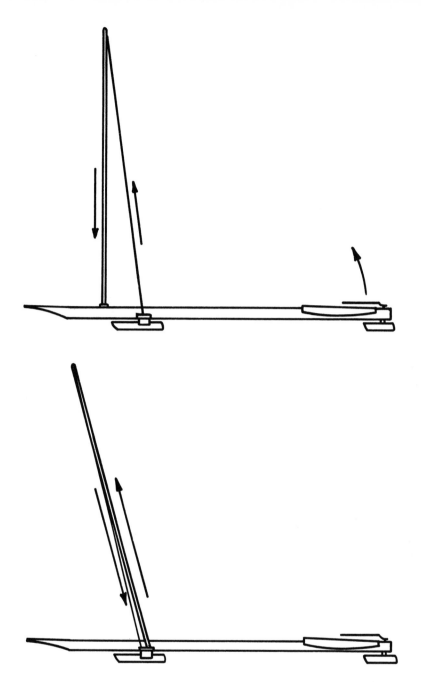

THE TEETER-TOTTER PROBLEM. Stepping the mast forward of the runner plank on the Hudson River type ice yacht solved one problem but created another. The center of effort was horizontally aligned with the center of lateral resistance (see preceding drawing), and thus the helm was balanced, but by being forward of the runner plank, the load in the mast (downward) forced the bow down. The backbone of the machine worked like a teeter-totter acting over the runner plank, and lightened the stern, reducing the grip of the stern (steering) runner. In the early 1900's, iceboats were built in New Jersey that had a mast leaning forward. The mast was bipod and the sail between was lateen (see following drawing). On these machines the load on the mast went directly onto the runner plank, eliminating the problem of forcing the machine down at the bow.

With the Hudson River ice being broken up, the centers of iceboating shifted to New Jersey, Michigan, Wisconsin, Minnesota, and Ontario. *Clarel* and many others of her type were products of the New Jersey fraternity.

One of the great problems of iceboating is that it depends on a climate that is not too common. The ice has to be clear of snow, and for this reason, iceboats can seldom operate on mountain lakes. Lakes in the Midwest are often covered with snow, but a good part of the time midwinter thaws will melt snow away or, failing that, wind will rake the lake clean. The Great Lakes themselves are almost never good for iceboating, because ice along their shores almost always shifts and packs. Iceboating is confined almost entirely to inland lakes or sheltered bays along larger bodies of water.

Big boats continued to dominate the sport until about 1930, when a dramatic change in design occurred and boats with only 75 square feet of sail were built that would outsail anything that was then on the ice or had even been on the ice. The design breakthrough was the bow-steerer.

Bow-steerers, like stern-steerers, have three runners. The difference is that the runner plank is aft, at the very back of the backbone, and the single steering runner is forward, at the front of the backbone. The mast is forward of the runner plank so that the center of effort of the sail (or sails) is over the center of lateral resistance. The advantage is that the downward load in the mast presses the steering runner into the ice instead of raising it off the ice, as it does on stern-steerers.

Wisconsin was the center of bow-steerer development. The first bow-steerer of any importance was built in 1931 by the Joy brothers, sailmakers in Milwaukee. With this boat, the Joys found out immediately that a bow-steerer will not flicker. The mast load is inside the triangle formed by the runners, and the runners always keep a good grip on the ice.

Others quickly picked up the bow-steering design, and a few large bow-steerers were built. Their success was various. A Class B boat (250 square feet of sail) was built by Starke Meyer, also of Milwaukee, and he ran away from everything else on the lakes. A Class A boat (350 feet of sail) was built at about the same time, and it was only moderately successful.

It was the Joy brothers and Walter Beauvais who came up with the machine that retired the big boats forever. Beauvais, of Williams Bay, Wisconsin, built a hull, similar in construction to the fuselage of a wooden aircraft, with two seats inside. The hull was 12 feet long, and an 8-foot runner plank was fastened beneath the back. The Joys built a sail for the machine of only 75 square feet. It went on the ice for the first time in 1933 on Lake Geneva, Wisconsin, and it was an instant success.

The machine, called the *Beau Skeeter*, was extremely fast, yet more maneuverable than any iceboater before could dream. Like the bow-steer-

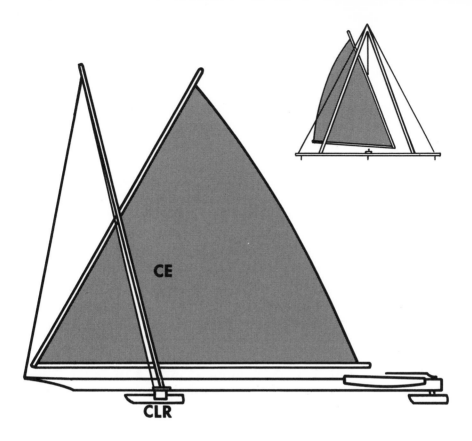

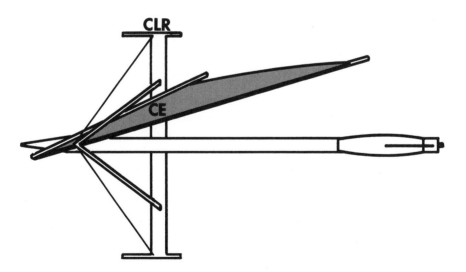

NEW JERSEY TYPE ICE YACHT. With a lateen sail inside a forward-raked bipod mast, ice yachts that originated in the early 1900's in New Jersey presented solutions to the two problems that had retarded the speed of the Hudson River type. The center of effort was horizontally aligned with the center of lateral resistance, and the load on the mast was directly onto the runner plank. The ice yacht Clarel, *for which a speed of 140 miles per hour was claimed in 1908, was of this type.*

ers before her, she would not spin, even while turning in a very tight radius. She was a tricky little machine, though, because she would hike at the slightest provocation and capsize from the hike if reflexes weren't quick.

From *Beau Skeeter*, a development class formed with the rules permitting anything of 75 feet of sail area or less. The first race was at Lake Geneva in 1934. The class is designated E, and the boats are called "E Skeeters" or "E Boats." Within the class there are subdivisions for two-seaters and single-seaters.

Though the limitation on sail area remained the same, the appearance of the E-class boats changed rapidly in the last half of the 1930's. The fuselages remained about the same, but developers drew them out farther and farther and they eventually reached a length of 20 feet, instead of the original 12. Runner planks also were lengthened, and by 1940 most were around 16 feet.

These skeeters with the longer members were even faster than the earlier skeeters. Just how fast skeeters will go is uncertain. There is a claim of a timed run in the 1930's of 146 miles per hour. Details of how the run was timed, except that a stop watch was used, are lacking, and the claim is given little credit.

Since ideal conditions of ice and wind are a hit-and-miss thing, iceboaters have seldom gone to the trouble to set up precision time traps. It was done once in the 1950's on Cass Lake, near Pontiac, Mich., with equipment borrowed from the Indianapolis Motor Speedway, but the wind failed to cooperate. All that the timers were able to learn was that an E-boat will go over 50 miles per hour in a 6-mile-per-hour wind.

A consensus of expert opinions and average of claims puts the top speed of E-boats in the range of 120 to 130 miles per hour.

Iceboating, like soft-water boating, has its one-design classes. By far the most popular one-design class is the DN, a very small machine that has 68 square feet of sail area on a 16-foot mast. It is 12 feet long and has an 8-foot runner plank. Like the E Skeeters, it is a bow-steerer.

The first DN was built in 1937 in the worshop of the Detroit *News* (hence the name, DN), by Archie Aarel, Joe Lodge, and Norm Gerritt. For many years activity in the class was confined to Michigan. In 1953, when there were only about 100 boats, the International DN Ice Yacht Racing Association was formed. Since then national regattas have been held in the United States, and in 1972, international championship races were held in Europe. The winner was Eindel Vooremaa of Estonia, which is part of the Soviet Union. Runner-up was two-time U.S. champion Jan Gougeon, of Bay City, Michigan, younger brother of the co-author of this book. The United States, Canada, and most of the countries of northern Europe were

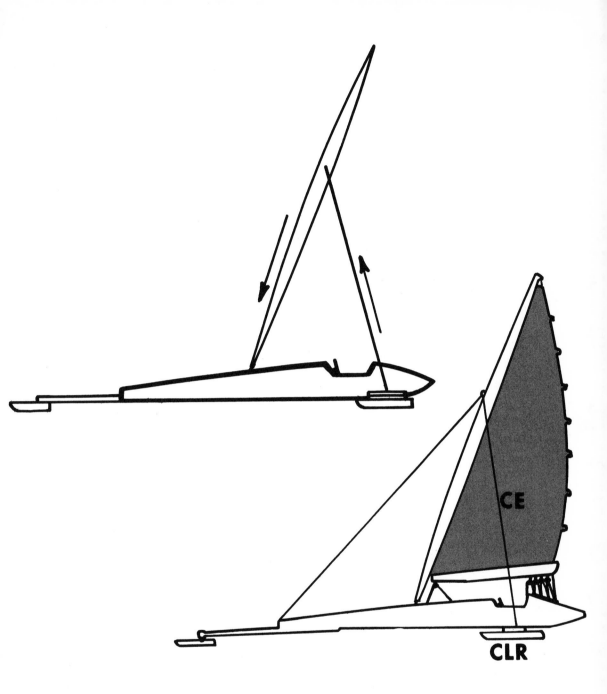

BOW-STEERING ICE YACHTS. The development of bow-steering iceboats during the 1930's ended all control problems, which had been the limiting factor in speed up to that time. Just like stern-steerers, bow-steerers have T-shaped frames, but instead of the top of the T being the bow, the bottom of the T is the bow. The advantage of the design is that the load of the mast (top drawing) is between the runner plank and the bow runner. Instead of lifting the steering runner off the ice, as on the Hudson River type, or having no effect on the steering runner, as the New Jersey type, the mast load of the bow-steering type presses the steering runner into the ice. With the bow-steering design, the center of effort of the sail plan is easily placed over the center of lateral resistance (bottom drawing).

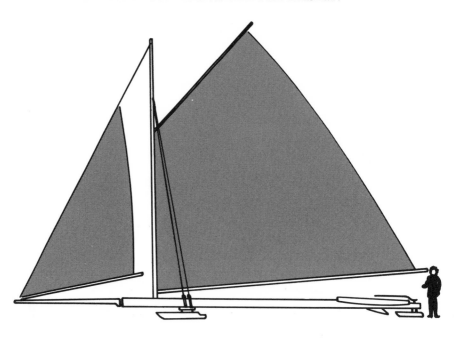

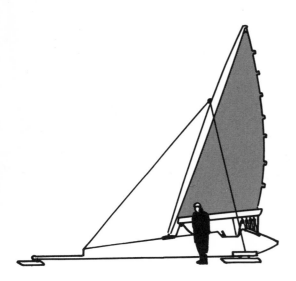

ICEBOATS GET SMALLER. Today's ice yachts, though they are faster than the old-time types, are not nearly so big. Drawn to approximate scale are a 50-foot Hudson River type (top), an E Skeeter (lower left), and a DN (lower right). The E Skeeter is by far the fastest of the three types. The DN is a one-design class iceboat of which there are several thousand in the United States and several hundred in Europe and Scandinavia. The DN can be assembled or disassembled in a few minutes and transported on a car-top carrier.

represented. Today there are several hundred DN's in Europe and about 2,800 in North America. The international championships are expected to become annual events.

The DN's are not terribly fast boats. Because of their extremely light weight (about 115 pounds in the most up-to-date models), the limit at which they can be kept under control is about 60 miles per hour.

The lightness of the DN is undoubtedly the reason for its wide popularity. They can be assembled or disassembled in about ten minutes and the components (the fuselage is the heaviest at 37 pounds) can be carried to the ice by hand. Two disassembled DN's easily fit on a car-top carrier.

Like their one-design soft-water cousins, one-design ice yachts have been excellent laboratories for increasing the power developed by sails.

VII Rigs for Outracing the Wind

For thousands of years it was assumed it wasn't possible to sail faster than the speed at which the wind was blowing. Iceboaters, probably in the 1800's, found out differently. We don't know exactly when, but somewhere back then the machines started outracing the wind—though the early iceboaters didn't understand why.

The art has progressed since the first discovery, whenever it was. Iceboats of the twentieth century have been timed in sophisticated speed traps at seven times the velocity of the wind, measured simultaneously with sophisticated anemometers. And just in the late 1960's, soft-water sailing boats have been developed that also will outrun the wind, though not nearly by such a margin. On one of these boats, a sailor sailing with the wind can smoke a cigar and leave his smoke behind. To sailors on clipper ships in the last century, even the idea of doing such a thing was so ridiculous as to be unthinkable.

Sails move, pulling boats along with them, because air pressure on one side differs from that on the other. The greater the difference, the more power the sail generates. Modern sails and rigging generate a much greater differential in pressure than old styles. How this has been brought about is the main subject of this chapter.

In the earlier boats, sailing was simply a matter of putting up an obstruction to the wind. The wind blew onto the after side of the sail and there raised air pressure a slight amount. What was happening was that the air molecules were piling against the sail and becoming slightly more dense than the surrounding air. The molecules, in trying to expand back to normal density, pushed the sail.

But pushing the sail away was not the only escape route for the compressed molecules. They also escaped to the side, billowing away from the center of the sail until they boiled off the edges and swirled around all across the front of the sail.

Eddies, or areas of turbulence, are worthless as a force for propulsion. Though there is some power in eddies, the air is just swirling in all directions at once and there is no way to channel the power in a single direction, which would make it useful. The pressures that do exist all cancel each other because of the multitude of directions. The net effect is that air pressure within an eddy is the same as in quiet air.

Normal atmospheric pressure is 14.7 pounds per square inch (psi). Any sail set across the direction of the wind causes air pressure to build up a fraction of a pound per square inch on the windward side. The leeward side, however, is all eddies, and pressure there, on the whole, remains at 14.7 psi, the same as the rest of the atmosphere. The sail is working on one side only.

Sails can and do work on both sides, however. Setting sails in certain shapes and at certain angles to the wind can result not only in pressure above 14.7 psi on the windward side, but pressure below 14.7 psi on the leeward side. The *differential* in pressure on the two sides determines how much power is generated.

Suppose that wind blowing onto a sail raises pressure on the windward side to 15.7 psi, or 1 pound above normal—a tremendous exaggeration, but convenient to illustrate the point. The sail is set across the wind and the lee side is eddying, leaving pressure there at 14.7 psi. The differential in pressure between the two sides is then 1 pound per square inch. In a sail that has 100 square feet of area, the power generated would be 14,400 pounds (the number of square inches in the sail multiplied by the differential in pressure).

Now suppose that pressure on the windward side stayed at 15.7 psi, but that pressure on the leeward side was lowered to 13.7 psi. The differential would be 2 pounds per square inch. Using the same formula, one arrives at a total thrust of 28,800 pounds.

This example illustrates that sail power can involve two factors, pressurization and depressurization. However, it is extremely simplified; the actual situation is considerably more complicated.

In the first place, the differential in pressure, even in the most efficient sail, never approaches anything near 2 pounds per square inch. We do not know what the maximum differential is on a high-efficiency sail, but we doubt if it ever exceeds .08 psi, and the maximum may be quite a bit less than that. Second, pressurization and depressurization are not the same all across the sail. The area toward the center will have much higher differentials than areas along the edges. Finally, pressurization and depressurization are seldom equal to each other. The figures of 1 pound for both in the example were used strictly for the sake of simplicity. The truth of the matter is that in modern sail rigs, leeward depressurization is usually many times as great as windward pressurization; 80 to 90 percent of the energy generated by a modern sail is the result not of the sail being pushed by the wind, but of the sail being sucked forward into a continuous, partial vacuum. There have been many attempts—none universally accepted as successful—to calculate the relative force of the two effects exactly, but it is enough for sailors just to realize that the leeward effect is the greater. Understanding this is the first step in understanding why sailboats can sail against the wind and also why they can sail faster than the wind.

Until the turn of twentieth century sailors knew nothing about atmospheric pressure, differential, and so on. Nonetheless, a great deal of improvement was made in sail efficiency just by trial and error. Even sailors in the ancient world learned to make their sails work on both sides.

When the Egyptians first got around to putting their masts in the center of their boats, getting the center of effort over the center of lateral resistance, they came a long way toward the technique of leeward depressurization. With the CE over the CLR a boat is ready to sail with the wind at either side or at the stern. In the earliest boats, which had the sail up over the bow, it was difficult to sail in any direction except straight downwind.

The first step in creating depressurization in front of a sail is to get rid of the eddies. This cannot be done when a boat is sailing dead downwind. It could not be done in the time of the ancient Egyptians, and it cannot be done today.

Then, as now, sailing straight with the wind is simply a matter of accepting the inefficiency of eddying and putting up more and more sail area as the only way to increase power. That is why racing yachts today use spinnakers on the downwind leg. A spinnaker is little more than a device to put up a big obstruction to the wind. It is a large triangular sail that billows over the bow. Only recently have sailors tried to flow air around them. They are very inefficient sails, but they are still the best way of increasing power when sailing before the wind.

To eliminate eddies in its sails, a boat must be on a course that has the wind somewhat off to the side, say about 45 degrees or more off dead astern. Such courses will permit the sails to be set so that air flows along them, but is not obstructed.

Blunt obstruction causes eddies, but air can be "bent" into flowing around a gentle curve without breaking into eddies. And air flowing around a gentle curve—such as a curved sail—develops much more power than air blowing against a perpendicular.

A curved sail that gently changes the course of the air has two effects. On the windward side, or the inside of the curve, air pressurizes. Air is made up of tiny particles (molecules), each of which has weight. When these particles are bent into the curve, centrifugal force causes them to compress against the sail, but as long as the curve is not too severe, they will continue to flow smoothly and will not eddy in spite of the pressure.

On the lee side, or the outside of the curved surface, the weight of the molecules tends to keep them traveling in a straight line while the curve bends away from direction of flow. The air tries to round the curve, but centrifugal force throws the molecules away from the surface. The result is that the molecules become thinned out or depressurized along the surface.

To a certain extent, square sails can be made to depressurize on the leeward side. The trick is to set them at slight angles to the direction of the wind and get the air to flow smoothly. Old drawings show that the Romans had discovered this. Square sails are shown with bowlines, a set of cords with the ends sewn into the side edges. The cords come together into a single line, which is pulled in order to flatten the sail. Bowlines were useful only for going to weather, when the sail was set more or less up and down the center of the ship. When the sail was set athwartship, the sides of the sail were outboard of the rail, and there was nothing out there on which to tighten the bowlines.

There were bowlines on both sides of the sail so that the leading edge could be stiffened on either tack. Bowlines were useful only for shaping a curve that allowed smooth air flow, and the fact that Romans used them is evidence that leeward depressurization was being used, even if it wasn't understood.

The fore-and-aft spritsail, another sail from Roman times, perhaps developed through attempts to smooth out air flow beyond what could be done on square sails. One of the main troubles with square sails is that the leading edge flutters, causing eddies. Bowlines only partially solved this problem.

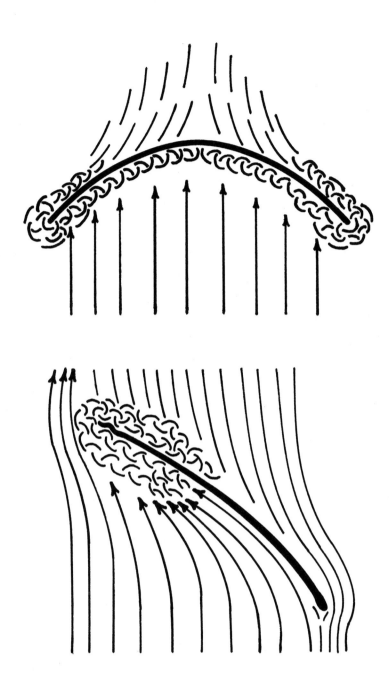

*AIR OBSTRUCTION VERSUS AIR SLICE. In the earliest days of sailing the meth-
od of getting power from the wind was to put an obstruction across its path, as in
the top drawing. The wind ran into the obstruction, a square sail, and broke up into
eddies, which swirled in all directions, destroying a good part of the potential power
of the sail. Before very long in history, mariners had learned to set their sails to cut
the wind at an angle, as in the bottom drawing, slicing the wind and bending its flow
rather than blocking it. Eddies were partially eliminated, and with the air flowing
smoothly over part of the sail, the sail developed much more power for its size. In the
twentieth century, new sailcloth and new rigging were developed that made it possible to shape and control sails with great precision and eliminate eddies altogether.
Sails today, for their size, are roughly twice as powerful as those of just a hundred
years ago.*

The fore-and-aft spritsail had a mast for a leading edge, eliminating fluttering. There also was better control of the shape. The forward portion of the sail (luff), which was fastened to the mast, could be kept taut, and lines from the top of the boom and the lower aft corner made it possible to tighten the fabric in all dimensions.

Lack of a suitable fabric retarded development of sails for centuries. Linen, handwoven cotton, and homespun were subject to stretching, sagging, and shrinking from moment to moment and from day to day. Even if old-time sailors occasionally happened onto a good shape, it did them little good because their sail material was so unstable that it couldn't be made to hold a shape that was designed into it.

The first material that even began to meet the requirements of high-efficiency sails was machine-woven cotton, which appeared about 1830. Because of the tight weave—much tighter than could be done by hand— less air leaked through and stretching was greatly reduced.

Shipbuilders, designers, and sailors, had they been given enough time to work with good fabric, might have come up with much better sails just by trial and error and experimentation. But unfortunately for the development of sails, steam engines, which drove the looms to weave cotton, began also to drive ships across the seas. Modern science and technology, which made it possible to develop better sails, also temporarily killed the incentive to do so.

The rise of yachting at the time commercial sailing was declining did not immediately lead to improvements in sails. The great designers of the time—Smith, Burgess, Gardner, and Herreshoff—found many ways of improving hulls for speed, of reducing weight aloft, and of getting ballast lower. They also found ways to put up tremendous amounts of canvas, but little was done in their times to improve efficiency.

Just after the turn of the century the sailing and racing of small boats started becoming popular, and the number of sailors in the world, which had been in decline, began to increase again. The new sailors and their boats were of different character than those of the commercial era. For the new breed, speed was a primary purpose of sailing. They had new things to work with, such as sail track, wire rope, even better fabric, and faster methods of sewing sails.

With this equipment and through sheer numbers of experiments, these dinghy sailors might also have worked out the precise shape of high-power sails, but as it turned out, they didn't have to. Modern technology, which had killed commercial sailing with steam and diesel power, provided a shortcut. Aeronautical engineers refining the airplane worked out all the principles of modern yacht sails. All that was left for sailors, designers, and sailmakers to do was to make use of the knowledge.

Aerodynamics, the study of the action of air in flow around solid objects, formally defined leeward depressurization as the most important force acting on a sail. It also defined the precise shape to maximize the force. The shape is called "airfoil," a curve that bends the flow of air without obstructing it. But the airfoil is not a regular arc. It is a curve that is rounder near the leading edge, becoming flatter toward the trailing edge.

Sails supported only along edges tend to bulge at the back. The friction of the air molecules passing along the fabric stretches the sail flat from the leading edge, moving any bulge in the material toward the trailing edge. The result is a shape that is just the opposite of airfoil shape, which requires that the full part of the sail be up front, the flatness toward the back. The task that awaited sailmakers, riggers, and sailors was to find ways to hold sails in an airfoil shape. Another task, every bit as important, was to make the mast an integral part of the airfoil shape and to seal the fabric and the mast, so that no air leaked through where they joined.

The shape of a high-power sail is similar to that of an airplane wing. However, a wing is positioned to develop its thrust upward, while a sail, being set vertically, develops its thrust horizontally. A plane wing depressurizes on the top and pressurizes on the bottom, creating lift that carries the plane up from the surface of the earth. A sail works the same way, but the thrust is directed to propel boats parallel along the surface. The direction of thrust is different, but the mechanics are the same.

It would be a poor airplane wing that had a big spar (no matter how light) fastened along its leading edge. The spar would form an obstruction to the air as it contacted the wing, and the air would break up into eddies, spoiling a great deal of the wing's lift. Similarly a mast, unless it forms an integrated part of a sailing surface, will cut down a sail's power.

Likewise, it would be a poor wing that had holes in it, allowing air from the pressurized side to leak through to the depressurized side. The leaking air would tend to allow the pressures to become equal, again spoiling lift. An imperfect seal between mast and sailcloth results in the same unhappy effect.

The changeover from old, wind-obstruction-type sails to modern airfoil types did not happen all at once like a startling clap of thunder. The change was gradual, over a period of about twenty-five years, during which sail design hung and wavered half in the past and half in the future.

The first step toward wing-type sails was the Marconi rig, which evolved about 1910. The Marconi was not long in becoming practically universal as the mainsail of small boats, and immediately with its development, sails started becoming taller in proportion to their width.[1] The basic reason rigs

---

[1] A term worth knowing here is "aspect ratio." The expression, usually applied only to Marconi rigs, refers to the relationship of a sail's height to its breadth (along the boom). An unusually high aspect ratio would be 6:1, an unusually short ratio would be 2:1. Most are 3:1 or 4:1.

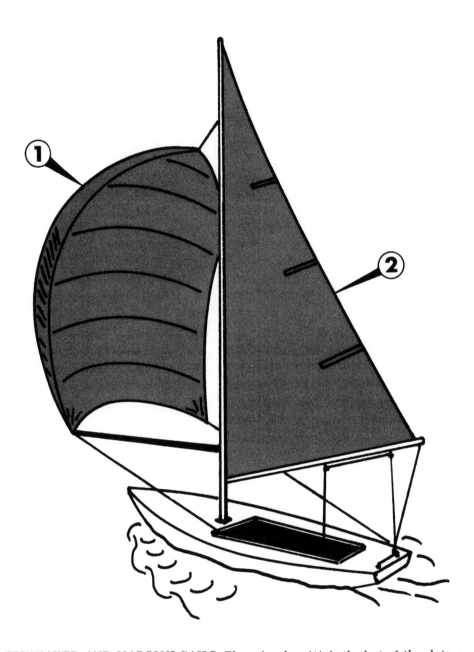

*SPINNAKER AND MARCONI SAILS. The spinnaker (1) is the last of the obstruc-
tion-type sails. Like square sails, it is basically used only as a perpendicular blockage
to the wind. Modern yachts use spinnakers when sailing dead downwind, or nearly
so. On any other point of sailing, the Marconi sail (2) is used to slice into the air,
bending it instead of obstructing it. In recent years, spinnakers have been developed
that can be flattened into an airfoil shape and used on points of sailing as high as a
beam reach.*

were made higher is that wind speed is generally somewhat greater up off the water than it is down close to the water. The higher a rig, the better it could take advantage of this source of extra power.

To increase sail area within given widths and heights, sailmakers soon began cutting sails with rounded trailing edges. A Marconi, if you will recall, is basically a right triangle, the two sides of the right angle being along the mast and the boom. The third side is an unsupported edge (the trailing edge) from the after end of the boom to the top of the mast. But instead of making this side straight, the practice that has come more and more into vogue is to round this side of the triangle outward, making the sail width more nearly uniform. The portion of the sail that is on the outside of the triangle is called the roach.

The roach is an area that is not supported by the framework of mast and boom, and so it has to be stiffened by battens, little strips of wood that fit into pockets sewn into the sail. The battens, which are made of ash and for a small sail are about the thickness of a yardstick (though not as long), extend from the edge of the roach inward, to inside the triangle of the sail. The stiffness of the fabric within the triangle, caused by stretching between the mast and boom, is extended out into the roach.

Though the sailmakers and sailors of the time may not have realized it, the battens along the trailing edge of the sail were giving a bonus in power beyond what was generated by the added area of the roach. The battens kept the sails flat toward the back and forced the fullness in the fabric to develop up in front. In other words, the battens forced the sail into an airfoil-like shape.

In 1925, Dr. Manfred Curry, a German scientist who also was a yacht enthusiast, published a book, *Yacht Racing: The Aerodynamics of Sails*. The larger part of the work is a treatise on sailboat-racing tactics, but a full third of the volume is devoted to detailing several years of experimentation with sail forms. That section, as it turned out, was a prophecy.

Dr. Curry was one of the top dinghy-racing skippers of Europe between the wars. He also had a flair for empirical observations, which he put to use to find out what made sails work and how they could be improved. His work included many dissections of bird wings, and he makes much of the close relationship between their form, the form of airplane wings, and the form of ideal sails. The book also includes the results of many tests with model sails (rendered in metal) in the air tunnel at the Junkers aircraft factory at Dessau. Other experiments of Dr. Curry's involved the use of smoke to make air currents visible as they traveled around sails.

Dr. Curry made several suggestions for increasing power in sails. He proposed using transverse (full-length) battens, battens that ran the entire width of the sail and were milled in such a way that when they were compressed by the ends, they bent into an airfoil curve. He suggested streamlined masts, the cross-sections of which would be the shape of a thin teardrop with the tail pointing aft, the sail being attached along the tail; and also rotating streamlined masts, standing on pivots so that they could be turned to bring the teardrop into line with the sail. He suggested overlapping (Genoa) jibs, jibsails of large size that not only filled the fore triangle (the triangle formed by mast, deck, and forestay), but also ran back along side of the mainsail. He proposed treating sailcloth, either by singeing or varnishing, to reduce its surface resistance to air. And he made many other minor suggestions, including returning the halyards on the inside of hollow masts (halyards along side a mast obstruct air flow); brakes for boats (flaps at the transom, controlled by a lever in the cockpit, that would enable a skipper to slow his boat without dumping the wind out of the sails); hydrofoil (streamlined-shape) centerboards; and streamlined shape enclosures for chainplates, where the shrouds are fastened at deck level, to ease resistance to water when the lee rail goes awash.

Dr. Curry himself tried out most of his ideas. He used full-length battens and the Genoa jib on a very successful 22 Square Meter racer in the 1920's. To get the battens to bend into airfoil shape, they were planed thin in the areas where it was desired that they take a sharper curve and left thick in the areas where it was desired that they remain more nearly straight. Full-length battens themselves were nothing new in the 1920's—the Chinese had used them for thousands of years—but the idea of planing them to curve into an airfoil was an innovation.

In spite of Dr. Curry's success with them, full-length battens are virtually outlawed in most soft-water racing classes and associations even today, fifty years after they were introduced. For the most part they are permitted only in wide-open development classes, such as Class C multihulls, where anything goes as long at it is not over 25 feet overall and has no more than 300 square feet of sail area.

Iceboaters, on the other hand, were quick to take up Dr. Curry's ideas. Charles A. Lindbergh, the pioneer aviator who flew *The Spirit of St. Louis* across the Atlantic in 1927, is said to have had a hand in the design of a very advanced rig that was put on an iceboat in 1930-31.

Lindbergh is related by marriage to the late Joseph B. Lodge, a Detroit millionaire who was a speedboating friend of Gar Wood and also was an international iceboating champion. Lodge built a series of Class A iceboats (350 square feet of sail and up) called the *Deuce I, II* and *III*. The *Deuces* were big stern-steerers on the order of the Hudson River types. They were not as large as Roosevelt's *Icicle* of the 1800's, but they were close enough so that they also had to be taken to the ice on railroad cars.

On *Deuce II*, with the help of Lindbergh, Lodge installed a rotating wing mast, believed to be the first ever used. A wing mast is a streamlined mast that is unusually broad fore-and-aft. It is designed specifically to become part of the sailing surface. The streamlined shape of the mast forms the sharp curve in the front part of the airfoil. Battened canvas then forms the remaining, flatter portion of the airfoil. The mast's angle of attack is controlled manually or "over-rotated" for best results. Generally a wing mast will not assume an angle that forms the airfoil shape if it is simply left to follow the sail's attitude, so some small tackle or levers are usually attached to the base of the mast so that its set can be controlled from the cockpit, independently from the controls on sail.

Deuce II was a hard-luck boat, plagued by rigging failures, as Lodge challenged for the Stuart Cup and the Hearst International trophies in the early 1930's. Most of the troubles were ironed out in *Deuce III*, a remodeled version of *Deuce II*, and in 1938 Lodge won both trophies to become champion of the world for Class A.

During the time it took Lodge to perfect the *Deuces*, however, Class A boats had been overshadowed by the development of the Class E skeeters.

The skeeters, because they are bow-steerers, brought a dramatic improvement in control and a much higher potential for speed. Wing masts and full-length battens quickly spread through iceboating in the U.S. Midwest after the rig first appeared on the *Deuce II*, and the skeeter builders were among those to pick up the idea. Even though they carried only 75 square feet of sail,[2] the combination of bow steering, wing masts, and full-length battens soon made the little E boats far faster than the big A boats, and interest in A boats was declining rapidly by the time Lodge got his going.

Dr. Curry, in his book, had suggested something on the order of the wing mast, which he called a "profile sail." The name is misleading, however, in that a profile sail was not a sail at all but rather a wooden sheath designed to encase a round mast and about the forward third of the sail. The encasement was, of course, streamlined in shape. The idea was tried on a few iceboats, but never caught on, probably because the wing mast achieves the same effect with much less trouble.

Soft-water boaters were not nearly so quick to take up the new innovations in rigging. While the rotating masts, wing masts, and full-length

---

[2]Technically, Class E skeeters are limited to 75 square feet, but the measurement includes nothing but the canvas in the triangle formed by the mast, the boom, and a straight line from the end of the boom to the top of the mast. Inclusion of the roach and the mast (which in reality is part of the sail) in the measurement would put most skeeters beyond 100 feet of sail area. Nonetheless, the point still holds that the skeeter is far faster on only a fraction of the sail area than the big boats which went before it.

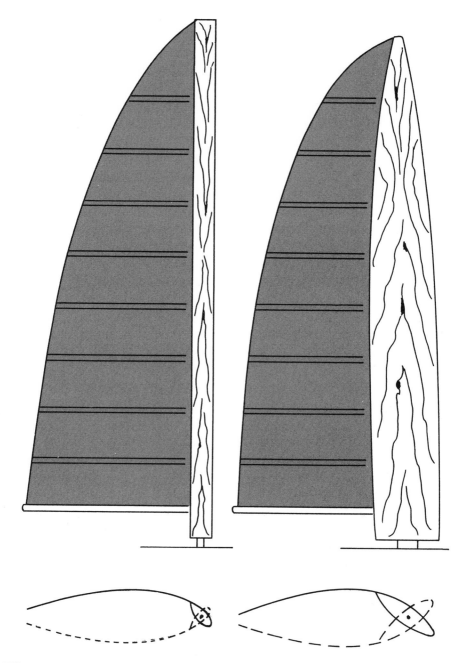

WING MAST AND ROTATING MAST. *A wing mast, shown with its sail at right, is very broad and may constitute as much as 40 percent of the total area. The wing mast and the sailcloth attached to it are designed to form a near-perfect airfoil shape, just like the top of an airplane's wing. Full-length battens stiffen the fabric, and the whole unit—mast, fabric, and all—is rotated for a favorable angle of attack to the wind. The wing mast is not very useful for everyday sailing, however. Even with the sailcloth taken down, the mast itself presents a great area of sailing surface, which is a distinct hazard in a storm. Similar to a wing mast, but not as nearly perfect a foil (and therefore not as powerful), is the rotating mast of streamlined shape (left). It is a narrower version of a wing mast and it is far more practical.*

battens were revolutionizing iceboating in the 1930's, staid old soft-water classes and clubs were busy protecting the status quo by outlawing the advancements.

Only a few soft-water classes of any size (in number of boats) allow rotating masts. Among them are the Class E, C, and M scows. The reason in those cases, no doubt, is that scows and E skeeters are from the same part of the world, Wisconsin and the area around, where a good many skeeter sailors in the winter are also scow sailors in the summer.

During World War II and the fifteen years after there were a lot of changes in boating. New materials and techniques of mass production had been feverishly developed during the war, and in the years following there was a boom in mass-produced pleasure boats, first in plywood, later in plastics. Whole new one-design fleets sprang up, based on craft with the new-type hulls.

Also coming out of the war were innovations in hardware, both in design and in methods of manufacture. Stainless-steel wire rope, which is practically impervious to corrosion, was introduced and soon became the standard material for standing rigging. Aluminum spars, which were expensive before the war, became inexpensive after it and many boats are now equipped with them.

Synthetic sailcloth, first nylon but by the late 1950's Dacron, became popular, and synthetic fibers also have now gone a long way in replacing natural fibers as material for marine cordage.

The greatest single improvement in rigging since the war has been Dacron sails. Techniques have now been developed to give the fabric a highly polished surface that has far less resistance to the passage of air than the best singed or varnished cotton, and Dacron is subject to only very slight stretching and shrinking. For years it will hold the shape to which it is sewn, and it is far less susceptible to rot and mildew than cotton. So superior is Dacron that today one rarely sees a vessel with cotton sails.

In spite of the availability of new materials, and in spite of a booming interest in boating, little was done after the war and even through the 1950's to improve basic design of boats or to put high-power rigs on anything except iceboats. The material and the techniques for building were new after World War II, but the basic designs to which they were applied had changed little since the 1920's.

Part of the reason that sailboat design advanced so little in the 1950's is that mass production encouraged standardization, both in boats themselves and in accessories. Also, although the trend seems to be the other way now, in the 1950's the public was much more interested in power boats than sailboats.

Also inhibiting new ideas was the fact that "ready-to-sail" boats were sold on showroom floors, with instant financing available in the package for standardized products. Not many people went to the extra expense to have an architect design a boat especially for them and then have a yard build it. Aside from the fact that there was a waiting period of several months for such a boat, there was the additional difficulty that such projects were more difficult to finance and required more cash.

In the 1950's there were some bright spots, however. Sailors of the time became very good at tuning up their boats for best performance, and the new materials made the rigging better than it ever had been before. There also was a growing interest during the time in multihull vessels, particularly catamarans. The catamarans of the 1950's were big, cruising types, built for ocean voyages. Their rigging was conventional, but nonetheless, many of them proved to be faster sailers than monohull vessels.

Some of these big catamarans were faster than others, and the idea of developing the hulls for speed became a fascination with younger sailors seeking bigger thrills and more speed. A movement got under way, and the International Development Class C (catamaran) was formed in 1960 to provide a common ground rule for racing. The rules of Class C are quite simple—vessels may be no longer than 25 feet overall and sail area may not exceed 300 square feet. The 300 square feet include the mast, the boom, and the roach. Even though the class is called "catamaran," trimarans also have been permitted.

Class C is a refuge for experimental machines that are barred from other races. It has been in Class C that the techniques and designs of modern iceboating have been adapted to soft-water boats.

The main annual event of Class C is the North American Multihull Championships, the first of which was held in 1961 at the Beverly Yacht Club, Marion, Massachusetts.

In the 1961 North American, Peter and Phil Ottking, brothers from Dallas, Texas, but former ice boaters in Wisconsin, proved conclusively that more power can be developed going to weather by putting the entire 300 feet of sail area in the mainsail, rather than splitting the area up between the main and a jibsail.

The Ottking brothers' catamaran had no jib at all, only a mainsail of very high aspect ratio on a rotating, streamlined mast. In spite of a rather poor hull design, which kept the Ottking catamaran from winning the North American that year, the rig proved far superior to the mainsail-jibsail rigs of the other Class C boats to weather, and experiments in the direction of the single-sail rig, or uni-rig, as it has come to be called, spread throughout the class.

A year later, Dave and Jerry Hubbard of Stamford, Connecticut, came up with *Sealion*, a uni-rig catamaran with an improved sail on sophisticated hull. With *Sealion*, the Hubbards dominated Class C for several years.

The wing mast, which became a standard fixture on iceboats in the 1930's, was introduced to Class C competition by George Patterson at the North American Multihull Championships in 1964, held that year at the Stamford Yacht Club, Stamford, Connecticut.

Patterson, of New Canaan, Connecticut, brought a catamaran, *Sprinter*, to the competition that year that had a single sail, nearly 30 percent of which was wood, the remaining 70 percent fully battened Dacron. Even though she showed great bursts of speed, troubles with the rigging kept *Sprinter* from becoming a serious challenge to *Sealion* in the North American, but immediately following the event, trials were held to select the boat to challenge the British Class C champion for the "Little America's Cup," the international trophy of the class.

In the trials, with Robert Shields at the helm and Meade Gougeon, co-author of this book, as the crew, *Sprinter* put up a strong showing, winning two of the series of five from *Sealion*. And though *Sealion* prevailed in the trials (she lost to the British defender), the day of the wing mast for soft-water boats had arrived, and they have been a dominant feature on Class C boats since.

The single-sail idea runs counter to the theories of Dr. Curry, who wrote extensively in his book of the "slot effect" of the mainsail-jibsail setup. Curry's idea, which is widely held today in all but the most advanced circles of experimental sailing, is that air is "bent," and therefore compressed, and therefore accelerated, as it passes through the "slot" between the mainsail and the jib. This higher air speed, so the theory goes, causes greater depressurization on the back side of the mainsail. The Genoa jib (a jib that overlaps the main) was all the better because the air could gradually be compressed over a greater length, permitting it to be accelerated all the more, Dr. Curry wrote. The Genoa jib has been considered especially important in going to weather.

No one questions that with the mainsail remaining the same, a rig is more powerful with a jib than without one, and that a rig with a Genoa jib is more powerful than a rig with a working (nonoverlapping) jib. The only question has been whether it is more advantageous, given a certain amount of area, to put it all in the mainsail or to assign part of the area to the main, part to the jib.

The question is still open, actually, but because of the experiences of the Ottkings, the Hubbards, and others who have followed, it is the feeling

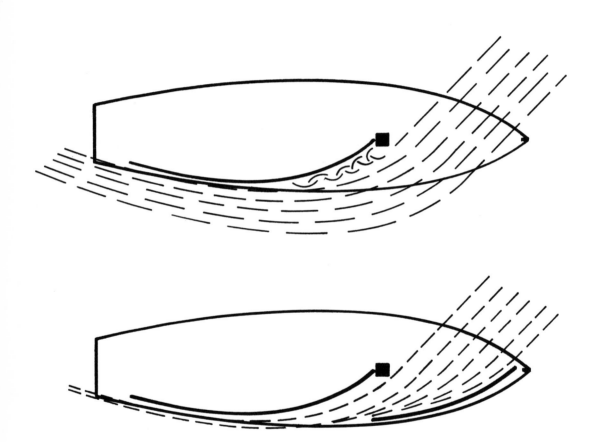

JIBSAIL SLOT EFFECT. According to the theories of Dr. Manfred Curry, the jib-sail increases the power in the mainsail because it compresses, and therefore acceler-ates, the wind through the narrowing "slot" between the jib and the back side of the main. While this may be correct for wind of low speed, the latest evidence from ex-periments suggest that the main contribution of a jibsail, aside from the power it generates in its own right, is to smooth out the flow of air on the back side of the mainsail. Stationary, nonstreamlined masts cause eddies to form over part of the length of the back side of the main (top drawing). The compression and acceleration in the slot apparently smooths out these eddies, bringing about an increase in power (bottom drawing).

currently that the single-sail arrangement is more powerful except in two cases: when the air is light, say around 10 miles per hour and below; and when the sail has a mast that does not rotate.

Above 10 miles per hour, the speed at which air passes is considered sufficient to operate the sail effectively. In lighter air, most feel that a jib is needed. The reason may be inability to control the shape of the sail when it has to be bellied out very full in light air; the efficient airfoil shape is lost. (Methods of adjusting airfoil shapes in differing wind speeds are discussed in the next chapter.)

A properly aligned, rotating mast and the sail attached to it together form a nearly perfect airfoil shape on the lee side, and air flow across this side also will be perfect. No eddies will form.

On a sail with a mixed mast, or even a streamlined mast that does not rotate, turbulence will be created in the area where the canvas and the mast join. Dr. Curry's arguments about "slot effect" and acceleration of air do have some merit for low air speeds, but at high air speeds, it is now believed by some that the principal advantage of a Genoa jib is to smooth out the imperfect air flow that is the result of a fixed mast. In other words, the feeling now is mainly that the Genoa jib, while it does create power in its own right, does not enhance the power of the mainsail at all except that the compression and acceleration of air suppresses the turbulence of a mainsail that has a poor airfoil shape. When the mainsail's airfoil is perfect, the rig is more powerful if the area of the Genoa is combined into one big main, or uni-rig.

Experiences with iceboats seem to support the contention that the single-sail rig is the most efficient. Except for a few novelties and anachronisms, all iceboats today, in fact all since World War II, have only one sail either on a rotating mast or a wing mast. Such rigging is universal on the faster classes.

Whether or not iceboats would be better with a jib in light air (below 10 miles per hour) is a moot question. Even if a skeeter or a DN were operating in wind of only 3 miles per hour, the boat itself would have no trouble whatsoever traveling beyond 10 miles per hour. Either with the speed of the wind added to or subtracted from the speed of the boat, the speed at which air passes over the sail almost always exceeds 10 miles per hour.[3]

---

[3]This phenomenon is generally referred to as "apparent wind," which means the combined effect of the actual wind and the motion of the boat through the air. Since iceboats generally travel at several times the speed of the actual wind, the motion of the boat has a lot more to do with the speed at which air travels across the sail than does the speed of the actual wind. It also has a lot more to do with the direction in which the air flows past the boat. On soft-water boats, the phenomenon is less pronounced, but still important. Discussion of the topic is included in the next chapter.

Uni-rigs and wing masts, while they are at present the last word in efficiency, do have some difficulties. The last word in efficiency and the last word in practicality, in sails as in other things, often differ. There are several arguments against the use of the wing mast on anything but experimental racing boats. First, very good materials and a high degree of technical skill are required to build and to maintain such rigging, and so, it is expensive. Second, wing masts and the accompanying paraphernalia are complicated, delicate, and generally less reliable than more conventional rigging. Finally, some wing masts make up 40 percent of the sail area, so that it is impossible to reef sail more than 60 percent without taking down the mast—no easy job on a quiet day ashore, let alone in a quick squall at sea. This last consideration alone relegates the wing mast to the status of a curiosity that can be used only in sheltered waters or near a harbor of refuge.

Even with all its canvas off, a wing mast still develops so much power that vessels that have them cannot be left unattended at a dock or on a beach. A little bit of wind will blow the whole vessel over. About the only way to leave a wing-masted vessel alone is at a buoy where it can swing freely around the mooring, and even then vanes have to be put up on the stern of the vessel to make sure that it always heads exactly into the wind. Otherwise the mast will develop power and either thrash the boat against the buoy or move it into a position where the wind can blow it onto its side.

The casual sailor who finds that he would need, say, 300 square feet to power his boat with a wing mast would be better off going to a more conventional rig, even if he had to put up 100 or so more feet of canvas to obtain adequate power. With a mainsail-jibsail setup, for instance, he would find the extra canvas a lot less bother than the difficulties he would encounter with wing mast.

The canvas of a mainsail-jibsail rig, being in two pieces with each of the pieces generating only about half the force generated by the one piece of a uni-rig, will require less tackle and less muscle to handle. One of the reasons that square rigging was used on big ships of the commercial sailing era was that the rigging provided a method of dividing the sail area into dozens of different sails. Larger sails would have been difficult to handle.

Limits on sail area are an artificiality of racing. Racing sailors must find ways to get every last ounce of power within a certain area of sail, but casual sailors are under no such constraint. If a more convenient and less expensive rig will do the job, then the practical sailor will not care that he is using a little more sail area than he would with a troublesome rig. However, if he is using a lot more sail area, just handling the extra canvas itself can be troublesome, and the same practical sailor might look for ways to get the same power, but reduce his rig.

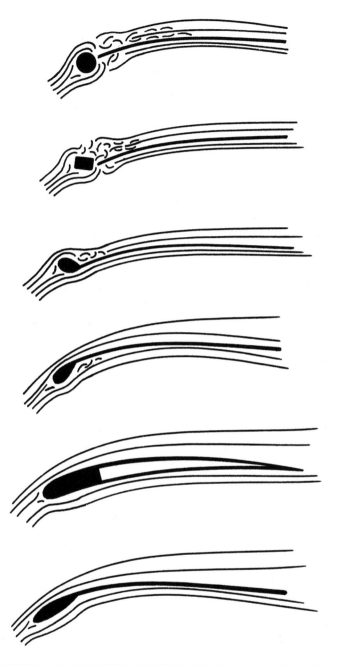

EDDIES CAUSED BY VARIOUS MASTS. Eddying causes loss of power in any rigging. Rigs that have a smoother air flow are more powerful for their size, making it possible for a well-designed small rig to drive a rather large boat. Shown in the drawing is the flow of air across mast and sail in six different types of Marconi rigging. Top to bottom are the round mast; the box-spar mast; the nonrotating streamlined mast; the rotating streamlined mast; the double-luff rotating mast; and the rotating wing mast. The nonrotating streamlined mast is probably the best combination of efficiency and practicality. The double luff sail (two pieces of sail fabric attached to a bullet-shaped rotating mast) is very efficient, but also very troublesome.

For reasons explained earlier, sails of high aspect ratio are more efficient —that is, they generate more power per square unit of area. In other words, an airfoil that is long and narrow is more powerful than a short, broad one of the same area; that is why glider planes all have very long wings with a small girth.

But extremely tall rigs, whether they have rotating masts or not, tend to have the same problems as wing masts. They are expensive and unreliable. While tall rigs are common on skeeter iceboats, multihull vessels are the main soft-water vehicles on which they are used. Like iceboats, multihull boats have a great deal of beam so that shrouds to support the high masts can be run at a much more favorable angle than is possible on a narrow, conventional boat.

Plain rotating masts (streamlined, but not wing) are probably the best all-round advancement in rigging since the evolution of the Marconi sail. When properly used, rotating masts become part of an airfoil. They are so much more efficient than stationary masts, which do nothing but hold up the sail and cause eddies, that a rig can be reduced by one third, and still generate the same power. In other words, a boat that has to have 300 square feet of sail on a stationary mast can go just as fast on 200 feet, or even less, with a rotating mast.

Rotating masts have been developed to the point that they are quite reliable. Iceboats and three classes of scows have used them since the 1930's, and practically all the production-line catamarans to come out since 1960 have been equipped with them. Failures seem to run at no higher rate than on conventional masts.

On plain rotating masts, which form very little of the sail area, there is no problem on reefing and mooring, as there is with wing masts.

The rotating mast is especially powerful when used with full-length battens milled to take an airfoil shape, and one such rig, commonly used on small, day-sailing catamarans, is very handy. The battens on this rig are all parallel to each other and to the boom. The sail and the boom can be taken off the boat together, rolled up together without removing the battens, and carried away to the car or clubhouse. On most conventional rigging, the battens are neither full-length nor parallel, and booms are not so easily removable anyway. To stow the sail of such a rig, the sail has to be taken off both the mast and the boom, battens have to be taken out of the pockets, and the sail folded and put into a bag.

VIII Aerodynamics and Draft Control

Sails, while they are ideally the same shape as the wing of an airplane, are much more complicated devices.

For one thing, sails have to operate on one side and then on the other, while plane wings do not.

For another thing, sails must operate in a very low range of air speeds (wind speeds), and they must be adjustable through a wide range of airfoils.

Airplane wings are not adjustable,[1] but airfoils vary from plane to plane

---

[1]Not counting flaps and spoilers, which aren't part of a wing's airfoil, there is one exception to this, the infamous F-111 fighter-bomber. The F-111 had swing-wings. When the wings were in the "out" position, the air passed over them perpendicular to their width. When the wings were "back" the air passed over them diagonally, which means that the air traveled a greater distance. Though the arch remained the same, the greater distance made the ratio of width to arch greater—in other words, an airfoil of higher speed.

depending on how they are to be used. A close examination of a cropduster, for instance, will reveal its wings to have a very full airfoil—in other words, the curve of the foil will be very high in relation to its breadth. The wings of fighter planes, on the other hand, will have a very shallow airfoil.

Cropdusters must fly—that is, the wings must develop lift—at low air speed, down to about 40 miles per hour. As air passes over the wing, an area of depressurization develops over the top, sucking the wing upward and keeping the plane aloft. The curve must be greater for air passing at low speed. That is why cropdusters have wings with a very full curve atop; and it is also the reason that sailboats in light wind will have sails set very fully.

Part of the depressurized area over an airfoil occurs in front of the top of the curve, and this area not only gives the wing lift, but *sucks it forward* as well. In other words, the energy created by depressurization is not vertical. The thrust is nearly vertical, but when the air speed is well matched for the foil configuration, the direction of thrust is just a little bit forward of vertical. The suction is actually working *against* the direction in which the air is flowing. That phenomenon of aerodynamics is part of the reason that sailboats can sail to weather.

The phenomenon only occurs when the airfoil is exactly right, or very close to it, for the speed of the air.

Airplane pilots can control the speed at which air passes over the wings simply by opening or closing the plane's throttle, or by going into a dive or into a climb. A sailboat skipper has no such control over the speed at which air flows over his sails. The air that flows over a sail is the wind, and the sailboat skipper must take the speed of it as it comes. For this reason a sail can operate efficiently only if it is completely adjustable through the entire range of airfoil configurations.

The wing of a cropdusting airplane develops its most efficient lift (lift that also has an element of forward thrust) at a very low speed. At higher speeds the area of depressurization over the wing moves back, farther and farther away from the leading edge, and as the speed increases eventually the lift is truly vertical. Beyond the air speed at which the lift is vertical, the lift develops a rearward thrust, or a thrust that tends to suck the wing backward. When this backward thrust increases to the point that it equals the forward thrust generated by the engine, the plane has reached its maximum speed. The plane continues to fly, though somewhat inefficiently, but it can no longer accelerate.

The depressurized area on a sail also will move aft as wing speed increases. The forward element of the thrust is destroyed as the depressurized area moves back along the curve in the sail and the thrust becomes

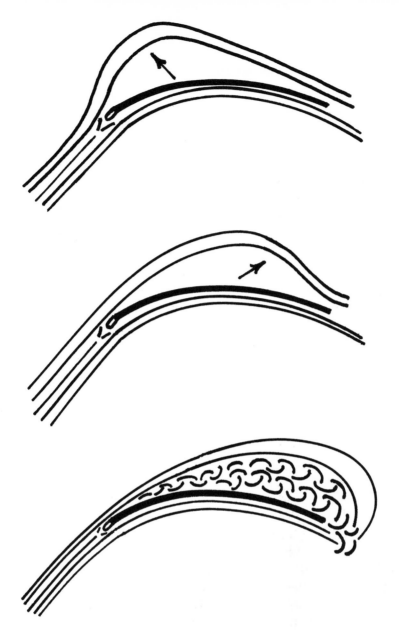

AIR FLOW AT VARYING SPEEDS. Over the same foil shape—be it an airplane wing or a boat sail—air flows in different patterns at different speeds. When the air speed and the foil shape are ideally matched, the air forms a pocket of low pressure toward the front of the foil (top drawing). Part of the power created by the foil being sucked into the low-pressure area is directed forward, in the direction from which the air is flowing. When the air speed is too fast for the foil shape, the low-pressure pocket develops farther back on the foil, forming a backward suction known as drag (center drawing). To correct this the foil must either be flattened or the air speed reduced. When air speed is too slow for the foil shape, the air eddies across the foil and develops no power at all (bottom drawing). To correct this, the air speed must either be increased or the foil made fuller. Airplane pilots must keep their wings (foils) operating efficiently by regulating the speed of their planes. Boat sailors, having no control over the speed of the air, must adjust the fullness of their sails.

directed more and more toward the side of the boat, causing a loss of power, but also causing the boat to heel greatly to lee.

The sailboat skipper does not have to accept this limitation, however, the way an airplane pilot does. The sailboater, if he has a modern rig, can move the depressurized area back up to the front simply by flattening the sail as the wind increases. In other words he adjusts the airfoil so that the curve has less depth.

A fighter plane, which is built to fly at high speed, has wings with a low airfoil curve. The depressurized area remains up near the front of the wing, keeping the forward thrust intact up to very high speeds.

There is another side of the coin, however. A fighter plane cannot fly slowly. Shallow airfoils, just like a sail that is pulled flat, do not work in slow-moving air. That is why fighter planes must have very long runways. In taking off, they must have a long distance to build up their speed to 100 miles per hour or so, and only at that point will the wings begin to lift. In landing, they must have their wheels on the ground before speed goes below about 100.

An airfoil's lift fails very abruptly when the speed of the air falls below the speed for which the foil was designed. As air speed falls to that certain point, the air just suddenly stops flowing smoothly over the foil and breaks up into eddies.

On airplanes, the speed at which lift fails is called "stall speed," and when lift fails, a plane is said to "stall." Stalls cause planes to drop very rapidly, and some planes also go into a spin. Pilots are taught to avoid stalls at all costs when their planes do not have sufficient altitude to regain speed and recover lift, because a low-altitude stall inevitably results in a crash. Boat sails also stall, but the consequences are not nearly so drastic.

The sailing skipper has an easy means to deal with a stall, however. When the wind lessens (the equivalent of a loss of air speed in a plane), a sail is merely adjusted so that it will be more full. In other words, the depth of the curve in the sail's airfoil is increased and the air continues to flow smoothly. Lift continues to develop.

In keeping air flowing smoothly around his foil, the sailboater has one problem that the pilot does not. Air comes to the plane's wing more or less always flowing parallel to the breadth of the foil. On sailboats, the air comes to the foil at an angle of about 45 degrees below parallel on all points from broad reach (the wind on the quarter) to beating (going to weather). When the wind is farther aft than the quarter, the wind has to come into the sail at an angle greater than 45 degrees, until, at dead astern, the angle is 90 degrees. The reason is that the boom can be let out until it is straight across the hull, but here it runs into the shroud and can go no farther. Very great fullness has to be let into the sail so that air being bent 90 degrees will be bent gently. Otherwise it will eddy. That is why spinnakers are extremely full sails. If a boat has no spinnaker, measures must be taken to adjust the mainsail into great fullness.[2]

A great deal of the skill of a successful racing skipper is his ability to adjust the curve of the sail to the speed of the air. The development of mechanisms to adjust through a whole range of curves, while holding the airfoil shape, has been the main accomplishment in sail advancement since 1920.

There are two basic devices for forming a sail into an airfoil shape, both described in the preceding chapter: tapered, full-length battens, planed precisely so that they will bend homogeneously through the whole range of airfoil shapes; and the wing mast, the angle of which can be controlled independently from the angle of the sail that is attached to it. The leading edge of the foil, the part which has the greatest curve, is formed by the mast itself. Only the relatively flat part of the foil, behind the deepest point of the curve, is of sailcloth, and this cloth is almost invariably fully battened.

Controlling the depth of the curve, or draft, as it is called, is a separate thing from forming the shape of the curve. The shape a sail assumes depends mainly on its battens, but also somewhat on the manner in which the sail is sewn.

Two devices for controlling draft, the outhaul and the bending mast, have been around for quite a while. There also are some recent developments.

The outhaul is the oldest device for controlling the belly of a sail. Loosely speaking, it is as old as sails themselves. Virtually every Marconi sail has an outhaul, whether or not it has any other draft-control device.

On a Marconi sail, the outhaul is a short line fastened to the lower aft corner (clew), usually by an eye splice through a grommet. There are some exceptions, but in general the outhaul serves two purposes: it holds the clew to the boom by being made fast to a cleat on the boom; and by the lengthening and shortening of the hitch over the cleat, it allows the leading and trailing edges of the sail to come closer together (in which case the sail becomes fuller), or it pulls the edges farther apart (which stretches the fabric in between, causing it to flatten).

The outhaul does a perfect job of controlling draft in the lower half or lower third of a sail, but because it works only along the bottom edge

---

[2]Airfoils are designated by a set of numbers, which are a ratio and a percentage. The ratio is the foil's breadth to its depth of arch. The percentage is the distance of the deepest arch from the leading edge. Thus if a sailboat skipper says he is running a "6-1, 40" he means that the depth of the arch is one-sixth of the breadth of the sail and that the maximum arch is 40 percent of the way back from the leading edge.

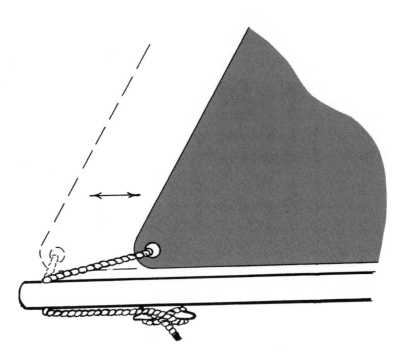

THE OUTHAUL. One of the oldest, standard ways of controlling the fullness of sails is the outhaul, which is simply a mechanism to tighten or slacken the sail by its corner. When the corner is pulled, the foot of sail becomes taut and straight. When the corner is slackened, the foot is loosened and allowed to become more full. Outhauls vary from a simple rope tie passing through the end of a boom, as illustrated above, to sophisticated hardware involving screw mechanisms and ratchets. Outhauls do a fine job of controlling fullness in the lower part of the sail, but have little effect on the upper half or the upper third.

(foot), it is not very effective in controlling draft up toward the top. The other devices, all of which are used in addition to the outhaul, are mechanisms used mainly to control the draft up toward the top.

The bending mast is by far the most successful and widely used device to flatten the sail above the area controlled by the outhaul.

Some masts bend aft, some bend side to side, but in both the principle is the same. The trailing edge and the leading edge are pulled away from each other, stretching the fullness out of the fabric in between. The mechanism is easier to visualize in the mast that bends aft, so we will describe it first.

Assume for a moment that a triangular piece of fabric, a right triangle in the shape of a sail, is lying on a wooden floor. The triangle is spread out, and a nail driven into each of the three corners. Also assume that even though the edges of the triangle are drawn tight, the fabric is baggy and that the center part of the triangle is loose.

Now imagine that a man comes along with a thin, springy board and a staple gun, and staples one of the sides of the triangle all along the board. When finished stapling, he then takes hold of the board in the middle and pulls it, bowing it away from the center of the triangle.

What happens?

The answer is that the triangle assumes a new shape. It is no longer a triangle. It is similar to a triangle, but the side fastened to the board now curves outward. And what happens to the fabric in the center? The bagginess is pulled out of it.

This is approximately what happens to a Marconi sail when a curve aft is introduced into its mast. Like the board described above, the bending mast causes the leading edge of the sail to curve forward, or to curve away from the trailing edge. The fabric in between is stretched and the sail flattens.

To describe the away a side-bending mast works on a sail, change the example slightly. Imagine the same piece of cloth, still nailed by the corners and with the board straight again, but this time the cloth is over a triangular hole that is about the same size as the cloth. The bagginess allows the cloth to dip down into the hole. The board is entirely over the hole except for its two ends, which are hanging on the edge of the floor near two of the nails.

Now suppose someone steps on the center of the board, causing it to bend down in the center while its ends stay up on the floor. What happens to the fabric?

Answer: The fabric takes a big curve along lines parallel to the board, but lines *perpendicular* to the board become quite flat.

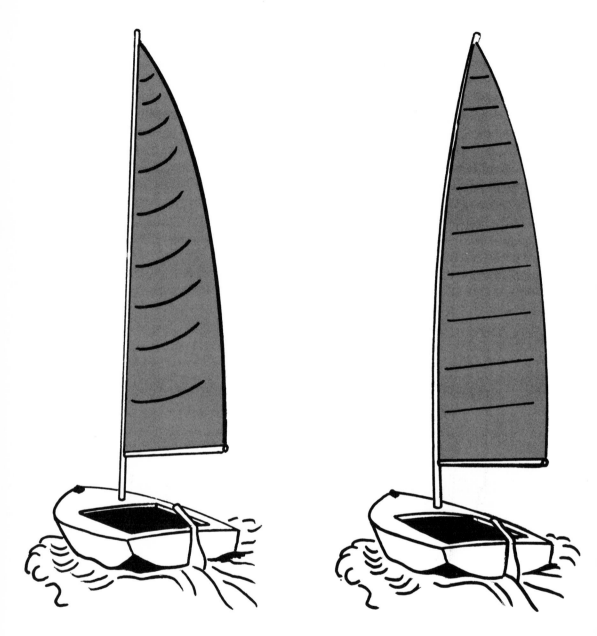

THE AFT-BENDING MAST. Inducing a bend aft in the mast causes a sail to flat-ten. Properly cut Marconi sails, when laid out flat, are not really triangular. Their forward edges, the edges that are attached to the mast, are slightly curved in an arc away from the center of the sail. When this edge is held against a straight mast, the curved edge is held in straight and the excess fabric being fed into the triangle makes the sail full. When the mast is bent aft, the bend matches the curve that was cut into the sail's leading edge, the excess fabric is pulled out, and the sail is flattened.

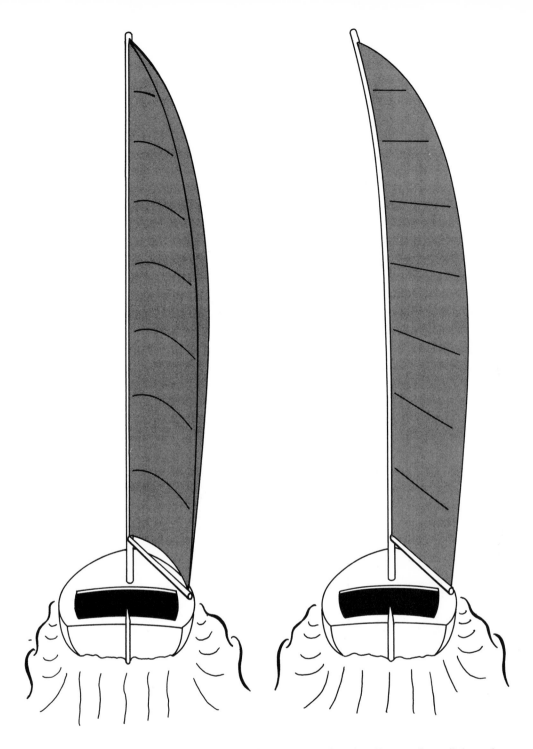

THE SIDE-BENDING MAST. *Masts that bend to the side flatten the sail by sub-stituting fullness in the horizontal dimension for fullness in the vertical dimension. Since air flows across the sail horizontally only, the practical effect is the same as if the sail had been flattened in both dimensions. Most rotating masts are designed to bend to the side, but since they are usually over-rotated—that is, rotated past the line of sail itself—they actually function about half as a side-bending mast, half as an aft-bending mast.*

Transfer this image to a Marconi sail, making the board a mast, and you will see that the lines perpendicular to the board are the lines that the wind follows as it passes over the sail. These lines are flat. The curve in the sail is *across* the line that the wind follows, whereas the only curve that influences the flow of air is the curve in the direction along which the air is blowing. In other words, the side-bending mast takes little fullness out of the sail; it mostly takes horizontal fullness and transforms it into vertical fullness. Horizontal fullness is needed for low-speed air. Vertical fullness is of no importance to either.

Though the mechanics of this analogy are correct, sails do not behave exactly like the fabric on the floor. The analogy is exaggerated, giving the impression that the bends taken by masts are quite large. For the most part, bends induced in masts are quite subtle. Also, in the case of the aft-bending mast, we had the triangle nailed to one spot in the floor. Actually when a mast bends, it is not bending from the middle, with the top and the bottom staying in the same vertical line. The top of the mast (and the whole top of the sail) goes aft. Finally, rotating masts, while they bend only to the side, actually take fullness out of the sail partially in the manner of an aft-bending mast. Rotating masts are always cocked at about a 45-degree angle to the sail, and therefore the bend in them, as far as it works on the sail, is halfway between an aft bend and a side bend. Allowances for this have to be made in the design.

What is the mechanism that makes masts bend? For a side-bending mast, it is the wind pressure on the sail. The heavier the wind, the more the mast bends and the flatter (horizontally) the sail becomes.

Building a mast that curves in just the right amount as the speed of wind increases is, of course, quite an engineering feat. Materials have to be milled closely, lest they be either too flexible or too stiff. Shrouds and jumper stays have to be designed and placed to keep the masts from bending too far, in which case they would fracture.

Another aspect of the engineering is to mill the parts and place the stays and shrouds so that the mast bends where it is wanted. As mentioned before, most of the belly in the lower part of a sail is controlled by the outhaul, so masts are generally kept very stiff in the lower parts and are designed to bend mostly up toward the top and take the fulness out of the sail up there where it is out of reach of the outhaul's influence. An important part of "tuning" a sailboat, something that racing skippers must do and that others should do if they are going to get the most out of their boats, involves experimentation in setting stays, jumper stays, and shrouds in various tensions until the right combination is found to control the bend of the mast so that the rigging will develop its maximum power.

Aft-bending masts are not automatic. They are bent and controlled manually as part of the operation of the boat. Even so they still have to be engineered and tuned in advance so that the mast bends where it is wanted. How much it bends is up to the crew.

The mast is bent by hauling down on the after end of the boom. The boom pulls down on the trailing edge of the sail, and the sail bends the mast aft.

The line that controls the swing of the boom is called the sheet. The sheet is connected to the boom through a block and fastened to the deck, also through a block. Wind pressure on the sail causes the boom to swing out, away from alignment with the center of the boat. The sheet is used to pull the boom back in and to hold it at the desired position. When the boom is "sheeted in" to the point that the blocks are aligned vertically, the boom is said to be close-hauled, which is the position at which the sail is set for going to weather. This works out fairly well, because going to weather is the time when flatness of sail is needed the most. Air speed over the sail is higher in going to weather than on any other point of sail because the speed of the boat partially adds to the speed of the wind.

On some boats it is considered necessary to be able to bend the mast and flatten sail on other points, when the boom is not close-hauled. For this, an extra piece of tackle, called a vang or kicking strap, is used. One end of this tackle is fastened to the boom, the other to the deck somewhere out near the rail. The tackle has to be removed before the position of the boom can be changed. An alternate arrangement, which is less effective but never has to be disconnected, is to have the lower end of the tackle on the mast, as far below the boom as possible. The boom and the tackle are then always in the same plane and can swing around the mast together.

Only older types of masts, either round or box spars, can be made to bend aft, so this type of arrangement is now used principally on soft-water boats with conventional rigging.

All modern iceboat rigs and the latest, high-power soft-water rigs have side-bending masts. Streamlined masts (whether they rotate or not) and wing masts are wide in their fore-and-aft dimension, narrower in their cross dimension, and any pressure applied to the mast will cause it naturally to bend sideways, across the short span, rather than aft, along the wide span. Aside from the fact that side-bending masts are less bother, because their bend is automatic once they are properly tuned while aft bending is manual, aft bending is incompatible with the latest design in masts.

Another device for controlling draft, the "Cunningham hole," is of uncertain origin, but it has been around for most of this century. The hole itself is nothing more than a grommet in the sailcloth right next to the

THE CUNNINGHAM HOLE. The Cunningham hole is a crude method of controlling sail draft. A sail has to be specially sewn with a stretchy material that is subtly bunched along the bolt rope (the rope sewn into the leading edge). The bunching allows the fabric to flow out full. The Cunningham hole itself is a grommet next to the mast and several inches above the boom. A piece of cord passes through the grommet and is looped under the boom. To flatten the sail, the cord is tightened, pulling the grommet down to the boom, and tied. The bunching is stretched out of the sail and gathered along the boom. The Cunningham hole is not well suited to precise airfoil control. Its usual application is to convert a very baggy downwind sail into a flat, weatherly sail.

THE LEECH LINE. *Among the recent innovations for controlling the fullness of the airfoils of sails is the leech line, a sort of drawstring. The line, which may be either of light cord or light wire rope, passes through a long pocket sewn into the sail. When the sail is full, the pocket is curved, with the center of the curve toward the mast. Pulling on the line causes the curve in the pocket to become straight, and as it does, it pulls fullness out of the sail.*

mast and a foot or so above the boom. A piece of cord loops through the hole and down under the boom. To flatten the sail, the cord is tightened, pulling the grommet down to the boom, and tied. In this way, fullness is gathered out of the sail and bunched at the tack (the lower forward corner of the sail).

Stretchy fabric and a special sewing job on the sail is necessary for the Cunningham hole to work very well. The sewing requires that the fabric be subtly bunched all along the bolt rope (the rope that is sewn into the forward side of the sail). The bolt rope also has to be of a stretchy fiber, such as nylon.

The Cunningham hole is used mostly on small boats that do not have spinnakers and have to use the mainsail for going to weather as well as going downwind. It is a crude device that lends itself to transforming a very baggy, spinnaker-type sail to a flat, weatherly sail, but it is not capable of making precise airfoil changes.

The leech line, a recent invention for controlling draft, is in effect a long drawstring. It is a thin piece of cord or wire that runs in a thin pocket sewn into the sail fabric. The pocket runs more or less from the sail's clew to its head (the corner of the triangle at the top of the mast).

However, the pocket is not a straight line. On its path between the clew and the head, it makes a slight, swooping curve toward the mast. To flatten the sail, one simply pulls on the line. The curve is straightened and all of the fabric between it and the mast is stretched and flattened.

Leech lines are not very popular because when they are drawn, they tend as much to cause a depression all along the pocket as they do to flatten the sail, and the depression causes eddies and some loss of power. Still, the depression is along the leech of the sail where it matters the least. All in all, the method works well and has the advantage of being inexpensive.

Builders of experimental sails who use full-length battens sometimes find it necessary to force the battens into a fuller bend. A two-way outhaul, one that can be forced in as well as pulled out, has been one solution, but another for the top of the sail is to use an inverted leech line. Inverted leech lines are exactly the same as regular leech lines except that the curve is away from the mast. Pulling the cord then compresses the battens, lengthwise, between the cord and the mast, causing them to take bow and increasing the draft in the sail. If anyone has used double leech lines, one to increase and one to decrease draft, we do not know about it. It is certainly possible, though probably seldom necessary.

The cambered wing mast has been used with limited success on Class C rigs in the past few years as a means of controlling draft in the fabric portion of the sail.

Wing masts themselves, as well as rotating masts in general, are methods of controlling draft. Either of these masts is almost always "over-rotated" about 45 degrees from the sail cloth. In other words, if the sail fabric is close-hauled, the mast will be cocked to where it is pointing into the wind. The fabric will be a continuation of the curve on the lee side of the mast, and the whole curve, in effect, has a certain amount of fullness. To decrease the fullness, the mast is set at a lesser angle to the fabric.

On a regular wing mast, the edge onto which the fabric is fastened is straight. On a cambered wing mast, the edge is slightly curved, giving the mast greater breadth in the center and less breadth toward the top and the bottom. The sail is cut to fit the curve. When the mast is over-rotated, the center of the curve pulls the center of the fabric more than the ends of the curve pull the fabric at the top and the bottom of the sail. The fabric is thus flattened at the center (or wherever the curve is at its greatest distance from the rotating axis).

The difficulty with controlling the draft in the fabric by putting a camber in the mast has been that the mast has had to be rotated beyond the point at which it would make a smooth juncture with the fabric. A sharp hump is formed all across the airfoil. The chances are that this difficulty will be worked out, if it hasn't already been. It is strictly a matter of finding the exact combination of camber and mast bend. The result should be a wide range of near-perfect airfoils.

Among Dr. Curry's experiments in the 1920's was an unsuccessful attempt to control sail flatness with a bending boom. Dr. Curry's booms were laminated and/or milled in such a way that they bent sideways,[3] taking an airfoil curve. The problem with them was that they took the greatest bend, allowing the greatest fullness in the sail, when the wind was the strongest, and took the least bend when the wind was light, or just the opposite of what was wanted.

The problem that Dr. Curry was trying to solve with the bending boom was how to get the sail to take an airfoil shape at the *very* bottom. Most sails of the time were fastened all along the bottom with sail track. Even when the outhaul was loosened, the sail for several inches above the boom was held flat by the track and only assumed the airfoil curve up away from the boom.

---

[3]Not to be confused with the side-bending boom is a boom once popular on iceboats that is bent downward in its middle, pulling fabric out of the sail in the same manner as the aft-bending mast. Down-bending booms are not popular because while they do stretch some fabric out vertically, they feed fabric back in horizontally, since the boom is shortened and the leading and trailing edges are allowed to come closer together. Though there is a net gain in flatness, sail shape suffers.

Dr. Curry theorized, and then proved in the Junkers wind tunnel, that sails would be more than 15 to 20 percent more powerful if the airfoil curve was extended all the way down. The bending boom was apparently his first attempt to accomplish extension.

Though he does not report that he did, Dr. Curry might also have looked at the possibility of eliminating the boom entirely. Gaff-riggers of the eighteenth century had loose-foot sails—sails with no boom at all, held only by lines from the clew, as is a jibsail today. With no boom, those sails took their natural curve along the foot, with the fullest part of the curve at the back. Aerodynamics of the twentieth century dictated that the fullness in the sail be forced up front.

Dr. Curry eventually came up with a partial solution to the problem that combined the best features of the two periods. He used a boom, but fastened the sail to it only at the outhaul at the very end. To assure that the sail would take the airfoil curve, he put a milled batten in it right next to the boom. The net effect was that the sail had *two* booms, one that bent (the batten) and one that stayed straight. The stiff boom could be used as a firm point to hitch the outhaul and regulate the curve of the battens.

Curry, and many others after him who have used this boom-batten setup, put the outhaul in its traditional position, in the very corner of the sail. This left the problem that when the sail took a curve, the pressure on the sail lifted the batten in the middle, causing it to twist. This final difficulty was solved by Meade Gougeon on his Class C trimaran of 1965. He moved the outhaul forward along the boom and attached it directly to the batten. When the batten took a curve, it actually crossed the boom at the outhaul, and though the upward pressure was still there, some of it was on each side of the outhaul, with the result that it was counterbalanced. The mechanism is now widely used on experimental rigs.

Dr. Curry felt, and wind tunnel tests sustained his opinion, that the sail would be more efficient still if the opening between the batten where it bowed out and the boom, which remained straight, were filled. Air working up through the hole caused eddies, he wrote.

Two methods were used by Dr. Curry to close off the hole. One was simply to cut a piece of canvas to the shape of the hole (at its maximum size) and fasten it to the boom and the foot of the sail. The other solution was to use a broad plank for the boom, making it broad enough so that the batten would remain atop. Later on Dr. Curry made the plank even broader than the maximum bow of the batten, so that air not only was prevented from coming up on the inside of the sail, but also was prevented from rushing up on the outside of the sail.

Such planks have fallen out of favor today because it is now felt that

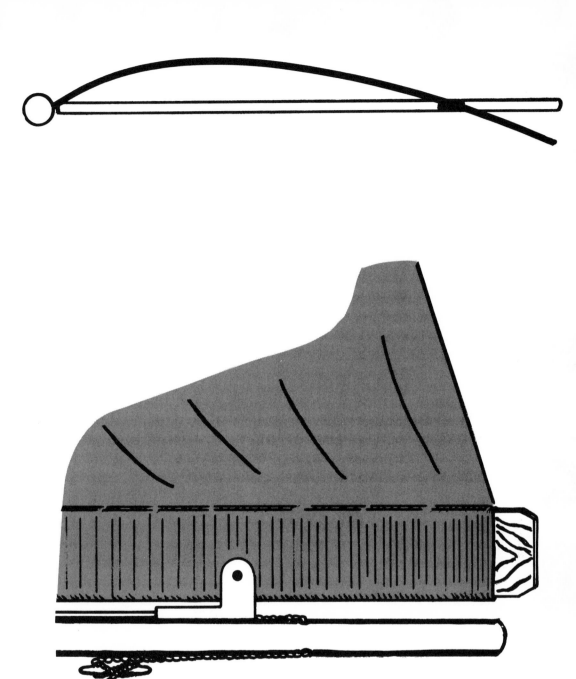

BOTTOM BATTEN INHAUL-OUTHAUL. Experimental racing rigs of the last half-dozen years use a heavy batten, milled to bend in an airfoil shape, all along the bottom of the sail. The curve of the batten is set by the use of a clevis that slides on a track mounted on the boom. If the slide is forced in, the batten takes a greater curve; if it is forced out, it takes a lesser curve. The slide is mounted forward of the end of the boom so that the batten, when curved, is part on one side of the boom, part on the other. With this arrangement, the force of the sail on the batten is balanced at the clevis.

they create more turbulence than they eliminate. In any event they are heavy and awkward, and Dr. Curry himself recommended the canvas insert over the plank boom.

In 1930, however, the America's Cup defender, *Enterprise*, had a plank-type boom that was dubbed the "Park Avenue boom." The Park Avenue boom was as wide as a sidewalk and it had dozens of pieces of sail track which ran *crosswise* on its flat top. The foot of *Enterprise's* mainsail was free to belly in and out by running on the tracks. The tracks, of course, were for the purpose of keeping the foot sealed tightly against the plank.

Today, sealing off the bottom of the sail in any manner is not considered very important. But Dr. Curry's idea that extending the airfoil shape down to the foot greatly increases power has proven to be exactly correct, and virtually none of the advanced rigs today have the foot of the sail fastened to the boom, except at the outhaul.

IX Catamarans and Trimarans

Conventional boat hulls have many advantages over multihull vessels, but the catamarans and trimarans have one overwhelming advantage when it comes to speed: They do not have to drag along tremendous dead weight to keep themselves upright.

Much of the history of the search for speed under sail involves the development of more efficient ballasting, because making ballast more efficient means one simple thing: less of it is needed. Less ballast means less weight to move. Less ballast also means less displacement, which mean less wetted surface and less water for the hull to take apart and put back together.

The colonial American schooners were fast, for more than any other reason, because the weight in the rigging was reduced from what it would have been had the vessels been square-rigged. The lightness above meant that ballast could be reduced below, making the schooners altogether lighter.

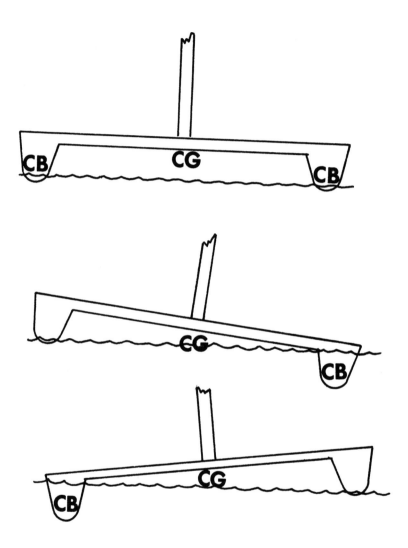

STABILITY OF A CATAMARAN. Catamarans are very stable boats because of the great distance between the center of gravity (CG) and the center(s) of buoyancy (CB). When a catamaran is at rest, as in the top view, the boat actually has two centers of buoyancy, one in each hull. Most of the force of buoyancy, which is an upward force, transfers to the low hull even at slight angles of heel, while the downward force of gravity acts through a center that does not change position within the boat. Because of the length of the righting level arm (the distance between the CB and the CG), even at slight angles of heel the craft has great initial stability.

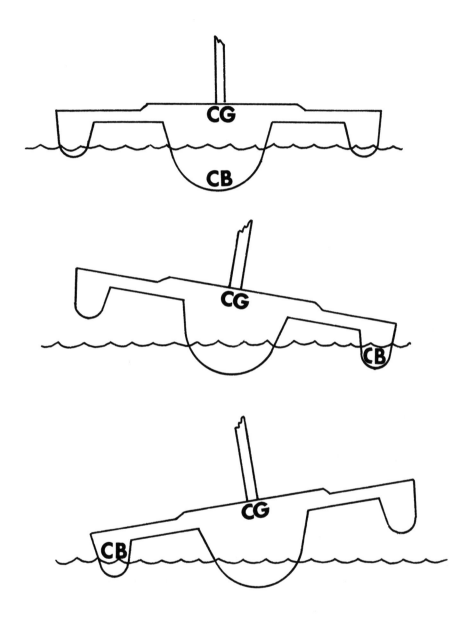

STABILITY OF A TRIMARAN. Trimarans, like catamarans, are stabilized by a broad platform of flotation. The broadness results in a long lever arm between the centers of gravity and buoyancy. Trimarans are in general even more stable than catamarans simply because they are broader. The great advantage of multihull vessels is that they are stable without the use of ballast. Without ballast they are much lighter and therefore faster than monohulls of comparable size.

Herreshoff scored a breakthrough in efficient ballasting with *Dilemma*, the first fin-keel boat, because the keel design got the ballast far below the hull, where it had maximum leverage. Because of the extra leverage, less ballast was needed.

Ballast leverage operates over a fulcrum known as the center of buoyancy, and the farther the center of buoyancy (CB) is from the center of gravity (CG), the more leverage the ballast has in pulling the hull upright. The CB and the CG may be separated either vertically or horizontally or both, but the farther apart they are, the less ballast is needed.

Catamarans, two-hulled vessels, have two centers of buoyancy, though only one of the CB's ever comes into play at one time. Each of these centers is always a long way from the vessel's center of gravity, and the boat is held rigidly upright even though there is no extra weight (ballast) hanging from its bottom. So stable is the craft that a rig of very high power (with respect to the weight of the vessel) can be used without causing the craft to capsize. The catamaran's high stability enables it to have a very high speed.

Trimarans, three-hulled vessels, are functionally similar to catamarans. Trimarans have three centers of buoyancy, two of which are far removed from the center of gravity.

Multihulls originated in the islands of the Pacific Ocean in prehistoric times. The first Westerners to see them were European explorers of a few hundred years ago. They saw several types of multihulls, among them canoes with single and double outriggers, proas, and double canoes.

The type first to be imitated in the West were the double canoes, which are the antecedents of today's catamarans. Sir William Petty, of Dublin, Ireland, built three catamarans from 1662 to 1664. We know little about them. The first of them was 20 feet overall, and we believe the other two were larger. The third one was lost in a storm on a return voyage from Portugal. The fact that she was sailed on an ocean passage suggests that she was a large vessel.

Like the multihulls in the South Pacific, Petty's catamarans proved to be faster than the ships of conventional Western design. According to Samuel Pepys, Petty won a wager of fifty pounds by using his second catamaran to beat the regular packet boat from Dublin to Holyhead.

In 1684, Petty built a fourth catamaran, a large one on the order of a small ship (the dimensions are unknown except that the mast stood 55 feet above the upper deck; the vessel had two decks). For uncertain reasons the vessel was a dismal failure. One of its known shortcomings was that it was difficult to maneuver, probably because of a great deal of windage.

All four of Petty's catamarans were experimental vessels, but from the size of his final one, it is obvious that he was thinking in terms of introducing the type into commercial sailing. As far as we know, no one before or after made any attempt to do so. All other multihulls of any importance have been built either for pure speed or for cruising.

Cruising multihulls, the big oceangoing types, have appeared in considerable number since World War II.

Development multihulls—racing machines—have appeared from time to time over the three centuries since Petty, but it has been only recently that they have been raced to any great extent. Since World War II there have been enough of them built so that they can now race against each other. Before then, and even today, they are largely prohibited from racing in classes with monohulls.

Nathanael Herreshoff, long before he was a builder of America's Cup boats and the like, experimented with catamarans. He built six of them, ranging in length from 24 to 33 feet, between 1876 and 1879. With the first of these, *Amaryllis*, Herreshoff entered the New York Yacht Club's Centennial regatta in 1876 and beat every other boat by a wide margin. His reward was that catamarans were promptly and permanently barred from club competition. Similar rulings met his other catamarans at other events, and he eventually gave them up to build steam yachts before turning to building the monohull sailing yachts for which he is best remembered.

Except for the gaff rigging, which was standard for small boats of the time, Herreshoff's catamarans were very similar to the designs of today. Unlike the designs of Petty and others between him and Herreshoff, the Herreshoff catamarans were constructed very lightly and the hulls were slim. Herreshoff took a stab at solving one of the nagging problems of the design, the tendency of the hulls to pitch separately, causing continuous torsion in the crossbeams. The solution Herreshoff tried was to fasten the hulls and beams by ball joints and use wire as diagonal bracing.

There is a close relationship between a catamaran and a scow. Scows might be described as two separate hulls connected by a wide, flat bottom. When a scow is perfectly upright, the entire bottom is in the water; but when the boat is under way, one of the hulls and most of the flat bottom are out of the water. The one-design scows now popular in the Midwest even have separate rudders and centerboards (bilgeboards) for each side of the boat. Scows are designed specifically to sail on one side or the other, and catamarans are designed with the idea that the two hulls will rarely support the boat equally.

G. Herrick Duggan, a prominent Canadian yachtsman and a construction engineer, designed three boats that successfully defended the Seawanhaka

Cup against American challenges in 1896, 1897, and 1898. The first two of these defenders were scows, and the Americans, many of whom disapproved of the type, gave in after being beaten two years in a row and chose a scow of their own to challenge for the cup in 1898.

For the defense that year, Duggan designed a new boat that turned out to be one of the most remarkable craft of the era. The boat was *Dominion,* a 37-footer that very much resembled a scow, but with an important difference. Instead of having the two bilges connected by a wide, flat section, Duggan arched *Dominion's* bottom upward in the middle until it cleared water, leaving the two hulls sitting separately with open air in between.

Dominion proved to be one of the fastest sailing machines of her day, and she roundly defeated the American vessel. Some believe she was the first vessel to "plane" (rise up in the water in the manner of a water ski). Many lightweight vessels now do this as a regular thing.

Technically (or actually) *Dominion* was a catamaran, and in addition to the Seawanhaka Cup, Duggan's ingenuity was immediately awarded the same prize Herreshoff got with his catamaran twenty to twenty-five years earlier—*Dominion* and all others of her type were permanently barred from further competition.

The situation for multihulls was no better in Russia at about the same time. Victor Tchetchet, who came to the United States to live after the Russian Revolution, relates that he built a catamaran and entered it in the Spring Race of the Imperial Yacht Club at Kiev in 1908. The boat easily won, but the racing committee disqualified the vessel and permanently barred it and others like it.

Tchetchet was an Olympic athlete for Imperial Russia and an aviator in World War I. Since the revolution he has lived on Long Island, New York. He is an artist and illustrator, but he also has a deep interest in sailing, particularly in multihulls.

In the summer of 1945, Tchetchet sailed for the first time the boat that is believed to be the first trimaran in the West. She was 24 feet long, looked considerably like a canoe with outriggers, and had a conventional sloop rig. She proved to be faster than other boats of her size around Long Island. In 1946, Tchetchet found a place to race her—in the Marblehead Race Week at the Corinthian Yacht Club in Marblehead, Massachusetts. She won a second place in the handicap division.

Two years later seven trimarans were entered in the Manhasset Bay Yacht Club's Race Week on Manhasset Bay, Long Island, New York. The trimarans ran in a special division of the races, but they had a place in organized racing and boats to race against for the first time since the *Dominion* was outlawed.

Tchetchet, who is credited with coining the name "trimaran," entered his machine in *Yachting* magazine's one-of-a-kind regatta[1] in 1952, but it finished very low in the standings and interest in trimarans waned. It was later to be revived, but for the moment it was being overshadowed by a renewed fascination with catamarans.

The potential of multihull vessels got a big boost from two materials that were developed during World War II and became commercially available afterward. The materials were the resin glues and waterproof sheet plywood.

The whole boating industry was changed by these materials. They made possible the production of light, inexpensive craft (both sail and power), which resulted in a boating boom throughout the hemisphere. The availability of the new materials was also largely responsible for the "kit boat" and "do-it-yourself plans" proliferation of the 1950's.

To multihull builders, however, resin glue and plywood meant a great deal more than saving money and labor. For them, the new materials presented an opportunity for great savings in weight. Stability without weight, after all, is the main thing that makes multihulls faster than monohull boats, and the speed of a multihull is related, more than anything else, to how much it weighs.

The catamarans built by Nathanael Herreshoff were very advanced designs, and in fact a replica of *Amaryllis*, built in 1933, has been officially clocked at 19.8 knots, though she needs strong wind for it. A few catamarans (and trimarans) since World War II have been timed at speeds approaching 30 knots. The highest recorded speed to date is credited to the 32-foot catamaran *Beowulf*, owned by Steve Daschew, of Los Angeles, in a timed run through speed traps at the Pacific Multihull Association's World Championships at Long Beach, California, in 1971. The speed reported was 31.7 miles per hour. The run was entirely on a beam reach. Highly efficient rigs enable today's boats to reach these speeds on much less sail area than that used on *Amaryllis*, but the main factor in the greater speeds today is that modern materials have made it possible for construction to be much lighter than it was with the techniques and materials of Herreshoff's time. The basic designs have not been improved all

---

[1]One-of-a-kind regattas are events for high-speed sailing at which competition is open. There are no restrictions on boats except that they be powered by sail, and so one-of-a-kind events have become favorite arenas for multihulls. One of the better-known of these regattas is held in the United States about every three years under the sponsorship of *Yachting* magazine, but there are many others of international importance held in various countries.

that much since Herreshoff, but methods of building the designs lighter have come a long way.

The new materials in and of themselves did not make multihulls instantly lighter. There was plenty to be learned on how to use the materials to the best advantage, and those lessons are still being learned. The problem is a matter of engineering—of figuring out stresses and strains, then figuring out ways to design and position a minimum of material to withstand the pressures.

Among the first to take up plywood construction of multihulls were Roland and Francis Prout, of Canvey Island, Essex, England, and Charles and Lindsay Cunningham, of Melbourne, Victoria, Australia.

The Prout brothers were builders of canoes and kayaks at the time they began experimenting with catamarans, about 1947. Their first effort in multihulls was nothing more than two kayak hulls fastened together with a frame. Power was from a lugsail and jibsail adapted from a popular dinghy of the time.

Even from the first the Prouts' catamarans sailed well. The biggest problem, and in 1954 they built *Shearwater II*, prototype for what was to different tack by turning the bow through the wind. But after several years of experimenting, sailing, and redesign, the Prouts worked out the problem, and in 1954 they built *Shearwater II*, prototype for what was to be the world's first mass-production catamaran. The Prouts began turning out the production model, *Shearwater III* (or just plain *Shearwater*, as they came to be known), and eventually sold over a thousand of them, mostly in England.

The production *Shearwaters* are 16½ feet long, 7½ feet in the beam, and weigh 255 pounds. The rigging is a mainsail of 115 square feet and a jib of 45 square feet. There are two rudders, one over the transom of each hull. The *Shearwater* is a very fast, comfortable daysailer.

The Cunninghams also began experimenting with catamarans right after the war. Like the Prouts, they started more or less from scratch, building everything to full scale and learning by trial and error. They first commercialized a design, *The Yvonne Cat*, in 1953.

The *Yvonne Cat* is a bigger machine than the production *Shearwater*. The *Yvonne* is 20 feet in length and carries 190 square feet of sail, also in a main and jib. Sails have full-length battens, perhaps the first catamaran so rigged. The performnce of the *Yvonne* is practically the same as that of the *Shearwater*, but if anything, *Shearwaters* are slightly faster in spite of their smaller size. Even though *Yvonnes* are bigger, waterline length is practically the same as that of the *Shearwaters*.

The most interesting difference between the two catamarans is in their hulls. A cross section of the bottom of a *Shearwater* hull is nearly perfectly rounded, similar to a cross section of a kayak. An *Yvonne* hull has straight sides, hard chines, and a V bottom, with the chines running below the water line.

The Cunninghams designed *The Yvonne Cat* perhaps with the idea of marketing plans rather than producing the boat themselves. At any rate, selling plans has been the main commercialization. For the amateur, the chine hulls are much easier to build because no compound curves are involved and sheet plywood can be used. A *Shearwater* hull, on the other hand, does have compound curves and has to be built up in molded plywood, which is sometimes tricky.

The Cunninghams and the Prouts developed *The Yvonne Cat* and *Shearwater* completely independently, without either knowing what the other was doing, and when the two boats eventually met in competition, a debate was set off among theorists as to what was the ideal shape for the hulls of multihull vessels. Beside the designs from *Shearwater* and *The Yvonne Cat*, other hull shapes from vessels that were never widely (or at all) commercialized were included in the debate, among them the flat bottom, with hard chines below the waterline, but flat across between the chines (Tchetchet's trimaran); the V bottom, with chine above the waterline (Morwood's *Gemini*); and the deep-rounded bottom, similar to the Prout design, but elliptical, the long part of the ellipse being vertical (Harris' *Ocelot*, about 1956).

The design that proved fastest and has become practically standard on racing multihulls is the round bottom developed by the Prouts. From a bow that is shaped like that of a canoe, a Prout hull is gradually rounded into a long semi-cylinder that becomes fuller in the middle and then thinner until it ends at a transom.

Round bottoms, whether on a multihull or monohull vessel, are the fastest for two simple reasons: they present the least amount of wetted surface for any given amount of displacement, and they have the smoothest fluid flow. However, a round bottom, when used by itself, is very tipsy. In other words it is unstable, like a canoe, only worse.

To gain stability, the monohull designer can do one of two things: he can keep the round-bottom design, but add ballast to keep it upright, in which case he pays a penalty in weight; or he can go to a flat-bottom or V-bottom shape, in which case he will gain stability without ballast, but will pay a penalty in wetted surface and fluid flow.

The monohull designer's problems are of no concern whatsoever to the designers of hulls for catamarans and trimarans. Multihull vessels get their stability because the hulls are set wide apart from each other, and the shape of the hulls themselves has little or no effect on stability. While design of a monohull is complicated by three factors—stability, wetted

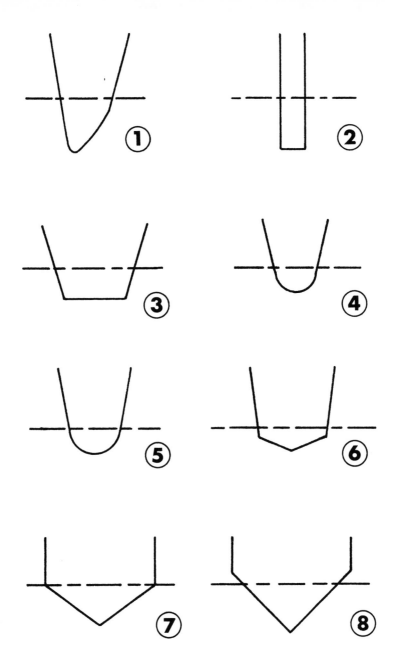

HULL SHAPES OF MULTIHULLS. Because catamarans and trimarans get their stability from having more than one hull, the hull shapes themselves have nothing to do with stability. Monohull vessels must have hulls designed to stay upright, but the designer of hulls for multihull vessels is free from this consideration. The hull may be designed with consideration only for speed. Among the shapes tried, illustrated in approximate cross-section are: (1) asymmetrical, Manu Kai; (2) rectangular, Lear Cat; (3) flat-bottom, Tchetchet; (4) elliptical, Harris; (5) round-bottom, Shearwater; (6) V-bottom with chine below water, Yvonne Cat; (7) V-bottom with chine at water-line, O'Brien; and (8) V-bottom with chine above water, Morwood. Of all the designs tried, the round bottoms of the Shearwater, developed by Prout Brothers, is considered the most efficient.

surface, and fluid flow—the design of hulls for catamarans and trimarans is complicated only by the latter two. With one less variable, the optimum shape in multihull hulls was worked out very early and the design is now pretty well established. Some designs offered to amateurs still feature V bottoms of different types, but only because they are easier to construct.

The ability to disregard stability has also permitted builders of multi-hulls to cut resistance in fluid flow by making the individual hulls very narrow in relation to their length. Just as in monohulls, the problem in fluid flow past a hull is one of taking water apart and putting it back together. For a hull to force water out of its path and then put it back takes energy, and the less the water has to be moved, the less energy it takes. Energy not used to move water goes into generating speed.

For any given amount of displacement, the way to disturb the water the least is to spread the displacement over a great length. There is, of course, an increase in wetted surface (which means a greater area of friction between the hull and the water molecules), but up to a certain point there is a net reduction in resistance when the hull is made very long and thin.

In designing monohull vessels, consideration for stability makes it impossible to increase the length-to-beam ratio beyond 5:1 or 6:1. Ballasted monohulls with narrow beam have very low initial stability. They heel far too easily and sail way over on their sides in the manner of the extreme "plank-on-edge" types in England in the 1880's. Unballasted boats with narrow beams capsize easily.

But again, none of these factors are of any concern to the designer of hulls for catamarans or trimarans. Just as the multihull designer does not have to worry that a hull with a round bottom is unstable, he also does not have to worry that a hull with extremely narrow beam is unstable.

The *Shearwaters*, which were put into production in 1954, had length-to-beam ratios of about 14:1 in each of its hulls, and many racing multihulls today have ratios of 20:1 or 25:1.

Specifically, *Shearwater* hulls have a waterline length of about 15 feet, yet at their widest point on the waterline, the hulls are only 13 inches. In Class C multihull racing, which permits overall lengths up to 25 feet, there will be many hulls with maximum widths of only a foot.

As has been explained earlier in discussing monohulls, a boat will displace the volume of water that equals in weight the weight of the boat. If the portion of a boat that is below the water adds up to a volume of 10 cubic feet, then the boat weighs exactly the same amount as 10 cubic feet of water. This is no less true of a multihull than it is of a monohull. However, the designer of a multihull is able to form the 10 cubic feet into a much longer and thinner shape. The multihull designer can make the volume about as long and thin as he likes, as long as it adds up to 10 cubic feet (or whatever the volume is).

On Class C boats, where hull length is fixed at 25 feet (maximum) and hull shape is rounded, the only variable by which beam has been reduced is by reduction in displacement. Engineering advances and techniques of lighter construction have resulted in Class C boats that are much lighter for their size. When the class evolved in the early 1960's, most of the vessels competing weighed around 1,000 pounds. Today few weigh more than 600 and some weigh little over 300.

The reduction in weight has reduced the under-water volume from about 15 cubic feet to something under 9 cubic feet in Class C boats. Since the hulls have been kept at 25 feet in length and the shapes have been kept rounded, the entire reduction in the cubic footage has gone to reducing the thicknesses of hulls.

Weight is a very critical factor in design of multihulls, not only because it is the controlling factor in the thinness of hulls, but because a given amount of energy will move a light object faster than it will move a heavy one.

Weight also imposes severe limitations on the use of multihulls as cruising yachts. Catamarans and trimarans become very slow means of transportation when they are heavily loaded, with food and extra crew members (and with fresh water, in the case of ocean passages).

The problem in the case of a vessel with thin hulls is that it will go low in the water, the hull tops will go awash, and the whole setup will become very inefficient. This problem can be solved by designing longer hulls, or hulls with more freeboard, or both, but then there is another problem—a drastic increase in wetted surface.

An ultralight multihull vessel has very little wetted surface not because it is a multihull, but because it is ultralight. Multihulls actually have quite a lot of wetted surface for their displacement. If you took the total displacement of any multihull and combined the same volume into a single hull of normal shape, the single hull would have far less wetted surface than the combined wetted surface of the two (or three) separate hulls.

But the multihull design permits a net reduction in wetted surface in spite of the two separate hulls because the separate hulls permit the elimination of ballast. The reduction in wetted surface through the reduction in displacement is far greater than the increase in wetted surface from splitting the displacement into two (or three) hulls.

However, as weight is increased, the advantage is lost. Because displacement is divided between more than one hull, wetted surface increases far more rapidly in proportion to increases in displacement than it would if the displacement were in a single hull.

In addition to the wetted-surface problem, there is another way in which additional weight kills speed. Lightweight boats, whether they be power or sail, monohull or multihull, tend to be lifted out of the water by their own speed. On certain types of small sailboats the phenomenon is called "planing," and one hears the term "planing hull," which is meant to imply that a hull is designed to lift itself out of the water. Some hulls are especially so designed, but the fact is that almost any hull shape will lift itself if there is little enough weight on it.

The speed of multihull vessels depends heavily on this lift phenomenon, which makes the hulls skim along the surface something like a water ski. The lift is reduced rapidly, however, by increases in weight. The hulls are forced to plow deeply through the water, resulting in great increases in drag.

The inability to carry even moderate loads except at slow speeds has caused catamarans and trimarans to be failures as long-range cruising boats except in sizes of 40 feet and upward. Theoretically a 25-foot or 30-foot multihull has enough room to accommodate and store provisions for a crew of four to cross an ocean, but as a practical matter the craft would be so heavily loaded that it would be little faster, if as fast, as a conventional boat. A well-designed and lightly constructed multihull of 40 or 50 feet can, however, accommodate a crew of four and still retain a great deal of its speed.

Speed is the main virtue of multihulls. When their speed is reduced to the point that they are no faster than monohulls, they become far less desirable in comparison. For one thing, a ballasted monohull boat is uncapsizable. Even if knocked flat or turned upside down, it will always right itself. Unfortunately, the same cannot be said for multihulls. While multihulls are very stable boats, a certain error in sail handling, can occur that can cause them to be flipped onto their tops. For someone far out at sea, such an event can only be described as a disaster.

Even if the crew or part of the crew survive the initial upset and are able to get up onto the bottom side of their vessel, the problem of righting the vessel without assistance is almost insurmountable. However, one way of getting the boat back up has been worked out. The first step in the procedure is to flood one of the hulls so that it can easily be submerged. Someone then must swim down below the boat and either fasten a line to the masthead or retrieve a halyard that is still through the masthead sheave. This line is then brought to the surface, taken aboard a dinghy, and hauled until the masthead is brought to the surface, in the process bringing the boat onto its side as the flooded hull sinks beneath the water. Air is then pumped into the flooded hull until it refloats, righting the craft as it does.

While this method of righting has been demonstrated in calm waters, we know of no case where it has worked or even been tried in storm-tossed seas, the condition in which a capsize is most likely to occur. And of course the method presupposes that the mast survived the impact of capsize.

The method also requires that a dinghy and air and water pumps and hoses be carried aboard for such an eventuality, and these items would add considerable weight, perversely increasing the likelihood that they would be needed.

Strangely, experience has shown, a heavily loaded multihull vessel is far more likely to be capsized by waves than one which is lightly loaded, another argument, and a very persuasive one, for keeping multihulls light in displacement.

A lightly loaded multihull has very little inertia for resistance to rising and falling with waves. Rather than plowing deeply into the belly of a wave, as a heavily ballasted or heavily laden boat will do, a light multihull (or any light boat, for that matter) will rise very rapidly and stay on the surface of even a very steep wave. When a boat is light enough so that it can stay on the surface at all times, the waves cannot board the boat or otherwise get a grip on it in such a manner as to cause it to capsize.

The possibility of wind capsizing a multihull can be minimized by prudent reefing and careful sail handling. Quick-release mechanisms for sheets, closely attended during the remotest threat, are musts for ocean-going multihulls.

It has been found that solid-wing multihulls—that is, multihulls that are decked solid from hull to hull—are dangerously susceptible to capsize under occasional conditions of high winds and high seas. As the vessel pops up over the crest of a wave the wind can get under the wing deck and flip the vessel over. For this reason, the hulls of most sea-going multihulls today are connected only by cross members, and the open spaces between, instead of being decked, are filled only with trampoline-type webbing or netting. The webbing or netting gives the wind much less to work on and greatly decreases the likelihood of capsize by wind.

The first modern cruising multihull was *Kamiloa*, a 45-footer built in the Hawaiian Islands by Eric deBisschop. *Kamiloa* was a conventionally constructed vessel, and the only thing remarkable about her was that she was the first of a great number of modern oceangoing multihulls. She was sailed from Hawaii to France in 1937-38, the first known ocean passage by a multihull since the ill-fated return run of Petty's catamaran between Ireland and Portugal, and probably the first successful passage since the prehistoric migrations of the South Sea Islanders.

Immediately after World War II, while the Prouts and the Cunninghams were working up their multihull daysailers in plywood, Woody Brown and

Alfred Kumalai were also busy with the new material, building an ocean-going catamaran in the Hawaiian Islands.

Brown was a former glider pilot, and Kumalai was a boat builder of long experience in Polynesian techniques. The result of their labors was *Manu Kai* ("Sea Bird"), a 40-footer launched in 1947.

Manu Kai was a tremendously successful boat and set off the present popularity of oceangoing multihulls. Because of judicious use of materials, through construction techniques and engineering from aircraft construction, Brown and Kumalai kept *Manu Kai's* weight down to 3,000 pounds, considerably less than that of deBisschop's *Kamiloa* and only about a fifth the weight of the 40-foot monohulls of the time, which displaced from 15,000 to 18,000 pounds.

Manu Kai was by far the fastest sailing vessel of her day—in fact—probably twice as fast as anything of comparable size. She has been timed on occasion at 28 knots.

Unlike monohull vessels of similar size, which need harbors and docks, *Manu Kai* operated off beaches around the Hawaiian Islands. She drew only 21 inches of water, and her wide-set hulls kept her standing perfectly upright when she nosed into the sand. The ability to operate off beaches (except, of course, in conditions of high surf) is a characteristic of all multihulls. Because they are light, many of the smaller ones can be dragged right up on the sand, completely clear of the water, where they may be left unattended. Some daysailing models are built so that they can be taken to beaches on car tops and assembled and disassembled on beaches.

Like the Cunningham's boats, *Manu Kai* was designed so that her hulls could be planked in sheet plywood, with the plywood itself forming a great deal of the structural strength. Aside from her construction, *Manu Kai* had an interesting design feature, asymmetrical hulls, which was to have a big influence in the subsequent proliferation of cruising catamarans in Hawaii and California.

An asymmetrical hull is flat on one side. If you took an ordinary boat and sawed it in two lengthwise, right down the center of the keel, and then took one of the halves and planked it up on the open side, you would have an asymmetrical hull. Brown built two hulls of this shape, set them apart, and connected them with beams and decking. However, the flat sides of the two hulls were on the *outside* of the catamaran, the curved sides facing each other beneath the beams. The purpose was to reduce leeway, enabling the boat to sail without centerboards.

Looking down on an asymmetrical hull from above, the hull would appear to be somewhat the shape of an end view of an airplane wing, or, in other words, an airfoil. In fact the hull is a hydrofoil, which works the same way as an airfoil, but the medium in which it operates is water rather

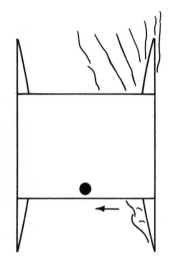
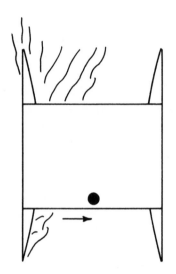

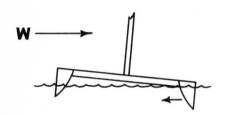
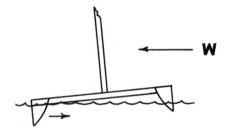

ASYMMETRICAL HULLS. Some catamarans, including a small modern daysailer, are designed with hulls that are planked flat on the outside, but curved on the inside. Looking down on these hulls from above, as in the top drawings, they appear to have the shape of the end view of an airplane wing. The asymmetrical hulls, as they are called, function as foils, and horizontal "lift" is created on their curved sides. The greatest amount of this lift is always in the lee hull, because the lee hull is the one that is forced deep into the water by the pressure on the sails. The lift then is always working against leeway and helps the craft make a course closer to the direction of the wind.

than air. Water flowing over the curved side of the hull is deflected and creates lift (horizontal in this case), which pulls the foil in the direction of the curve.

Catamarans, unless they are sailing dead downwind, ride much more heavily on the lee hull than on the weather hull. They do not heel very much, as a monohull boat does, but there is a great pressure for them to ride down on the lee side just the same. The result is that the lee hull will run deeper than the weather hull and will develop lift. The direction of the lift is to weather, therefore reducing leeway.

Asymmetrical hulls have not remained popular. Considerations for wetted surface and fluid flow have influenced recent designers to give up the idea in favor of centerboards or daggerboards on the assumption that in so doing their boats will be faster. The assumption appears to be correct, but on top of that is the fact that asymmetrical hulls are rarely, by themselves, adequate means for lateral resistance, so that boats with asymmetrical hulls will usually have to have centerboards anyway. There also is the fact that symmetrical hulls with semicircular sections are better in planing for the simple reason that they present a broader bottom surface to the water.

On the side of asymmetrical hulls is that they can be used to give ride, an important consideration on cruising catamarans. Any hull that is narrow in proportion to its breadth, all else being equal, will run deeper. But unless the hull has some abrupt flare on or about the waterline it will rise and fall very gently in waves. Wide, flat-bottom hulls, and to a lesser extent round-bottom hulls, have a rather rigid resistance to even slight submersion. The result is that they react very quickly in rising on waves and therefore give a bumpy or jerky ride, which puts some extra strain on the structure and, over a long voyage, puts a noticeable strain on people aboard. Deep-running hulls are a solution to that problem, and asymmetry is a worthwhile design if hulls are going to be made deep-running anyway, for in that circumstance there would be little penalty in wetted surface, and running at depth they would be very effective in cutting down leeway.

The trimaran movement, which flared briefly under Victor Tchetchet and then went into limbo again about 1950, was reawakened ten years later through the designs and the salesmanship of Arthur Piver of Mill Valley, California.

Piver was a yachtsman, a publisher of trade journals by profession and an amateur designer. In the 1950's he was interested in catamarans, but he then turned to trimarans. He gained some recognition in 1960 when he made the first known voyage across the Atlantic in a trimaran.

The crossing was in a boat called *Nimble*, a 30-footer built in California and then trucked across the United States to Massachusetts. Piver was trying to get *Nimble* to England so that he could sail her back as an entry in the Trans-Atlantic Single Handers' Race, which was starting from Plymouth that summer. He failed to get to Plymouth in time for the start, but the crossing nonetheless earned him a measure of fame and for the first time focused attention on trimarans as seagoing multihulls, a field up to which time had been the exclusive domain of catamarans.

Following the Atlantic crossing Piver went heavily into the business of selling plans for his designs, which ranged in length from 25 to 60 feet. He ran advertising in numerous boating publications, eventually wrote three books, and lectured widely to dispel prejudices against trimarans as ocean vessels.

Piver was a marvelous salesman, and in the 1960's his plans were sold far and wide. He also was a man of boundless energy. In the summer of 1961, just one year after his Atlantic crossing, he made the first crossing of the Pacific in a modern trimaran, sailing the 35-foot *Lodestar* from San Francisco to Los Angeles, Hawaii, Tahiti, and Auckland, New Zealand. On the first leg of the crossing, *Lodestar*, with Piver aboard, and another Piver trimaran, which was of the *Nimble* type, were unofficially competing in the annual monohull race from Los Angeles to Hawaii. Both trimarans beat several of the larger monohulls, and it is felt that *Lodestar* could have beaten many more or perhaps all of them except that she was under-rigged.

In the early part of his career Piver was little interested in making his designs competitive in speed with monohulls. His boats were characteristically heavily constructed and lightly rigged. His sales appeal was to the amateur, and his pitch was economy, ease of construction, and safety at sea. All of the plans that he offered were designs that could be planked in sheet plywood. He designed for and recommended the use of materials that could be procured inexpensively from local lumberyards. Some of Piver's economies were shortsighted—inferior materials are certain to hurt the longevity of a boat—but on the whole his money-saving ideas were well thought out.

Along toward the end of his career, Piver was forced to go into designs for more speed. Several others had entered the field of designing cruising trimarans by 1965 and speed had become an important selling point.

Piver's last boat, the 33-foot *Stiletto*, was perhaps his masterpiece. At any rate she proved to be far faster in competition than any of his earlier boats. In 1966 he sailed her to the East Coast of the United States, where she easily won the First World Multihull Championship off Long Island, and then he sailed her on to England, his second and last crossing of the Atlantic. Piver left *Stiletto* at Brightlingsea, to have her there for the 1968 Single Handers' Trans-Atlantic Race, and flew back to the United States. One of the rules of the race is that every skipper has to have previously sailed a 50-mile, nonstop, single-handed ocean passage. To qualify under this rule, Piver sailed from San Francisco alone, bound for San Diego, in March of 1968, in a 25-foot *Nugget*. He never showed up in San Diego, and neither his body nor any trace of his boat was ever found.

Dozens of designers and builders from all over the world have come along since Piver first opened the field of cruising trimarans, and great improvements have evolved. However, in regard to performance, there is little to be said that has not been described earlier in this chapter in connection with catamarans—hulls have become longer and thinner as construction has become lighter; the huge, V-bottom outrigging hulls espoused by Piver have now largely fallen out of favor and smaller, round-bottom hulls have been adopted; and so on. Molded-plywood construction is now very common in trimaran construction, just as it has been for a long time in catamarans.

An ongoing argument in design is the submersible versus the nonsubmersible outrigging hull. The latter is a hull that has enough buoyancy (is large enough) so that it will support the entire weight of the vessel, while the former will not. At the bottom of the argument is the question: When the wind overpowers a vessel, is it more desirable that the outrigging hull go beneath the water, or that the main hull rise off the water?

All of Piver's designs had massive outrigging hulls that were nonsubmersible. Two Australians, the late Headley Nicol and, afterward, Locke Crowther, were the original proponents of the submersible hulls.

The original objections to submersible hulls were that they were inefficient, that wetted surface increased tremendously and fluid flow was disrupted when the hull plowed deeply through waves. While there is merit in these arguments, there is also quite a bit to be said for submersible hulls.

First, they provide a clear-cut warning of when sail should be reduced. When the lee hull consistently rides low in the water, the meaning is that the boat is carrying too much sail and is in danger of a capsize. Fully buoyant hulls provide no such warning. Second, in a sudden puff of wind that could capsize the vessel, the hull will submerge rather slowly, allowing the crew time to dump air out of the sails to right the craft. Third, in conditions where there is no danger (or little danger) of capsize, submersible hulls provide a more buoyant ride, which is easier on the structure and on the people aboard.

The controversy is not yet resolved, but at present, hulls that are submersible, though only barely so, seem to have the best of the argument.

A new technique in construction—the fiberglass sandwich—was developed in the 1960's and has been applied to both catamarans and trimarans. Solid fiberglass, such as is now used throughout the monohull sailing and power boat industries, is too heavy a material for multihulls when used in enough thickness to have structural integrity. However, molded fiberglass has been used in two thin layers to sandwich a core of very light material. It was first done with end-grain balsa wood as the core material in the early 1960's by Tom Urie, of Port Isabel, Texas, who is in the business of molding Piver designs with his method.

In 1965, Derek Kelsall, an Englishman who was the first to sail a multi-hull in the Trans-Atlantic Single Handers' Race in 1964, built a trimaran the following year that had a polyvinyl chloride foam core between layers of fiberglass. The trimaran was *Toria*, a 42-footer that had proven herself to be very fast. Aside from her breakthrough in construction she was the first large trimaran known to have round-bottom hulls.

Polyvinyl chloride foam is a rigid material that adheres to the fiberglass in which it is encased. All the individual cells in the foam are water-sealed against each other, so that if there is some kind of leak in the sandwich the core cannot soak up water.

One of the bigger problems with sandwich-core hulls of any type is shear, the working of the two shells of fibergass against each other in stress. Such workings are so slight as to be imperceptible, yet they can cause the core shells to delaminate. The problem has largely been solved, and sandwich hulls are now commonly found on production-line monohulls, though they would be a difficult item for amateur construction.

Kelsall was not the first to use the foam-sandwich construction, but he was the first to make a reasonable success of it, and he apparently was the first to use it for a large-size multihull. Whether or not it originated in the United States, the Americans in Class C competition relied heavily on the foam-sandwich idea, and in fact American catamarans that have raced for the "Little America's Cup," the world Class C trophy, mostly have been of the sandwich variety. The main problem with them was a short life span because of delamination.

One of the big problems for owners of large multihulls, especially trimarans, has been that they take up a lot of room in a harbor. Owners of multihulls find themselves having to pay double or triple for a berth simply because their boat will take up slips that would accommodate two or three monohulls of the same length.

An English designer, John Westell, of Totnes, Devan, Kent, has been designing trimarans that "fold up." Connecting the main hull and the out-rigging hull are beams that are on hinges at each end. For the harbor, the outrigging hulls and the beams are folded aft, into the side of the main hull. At sea, when the beams are straight out, diagonal bracing is fastened between the four hinges to make the structure rigid. The obvious problem is strength in the hinge joints, but Westell has worked it out very well and has had several successful boats with the design.

An all-new concept in multihull design, or at least all-new in modern terms, came off the drawing board of Dick Newick, a naval architect of Christiansted, St. Croix, U. S. Virgin Islands. Actually the basic design has been used for several thousand years in the islands of the Pacific, but Newick was, as far as we know, the first to build a modern version.

Newick's boat was *Cheers*, a proa, built specifically for the Trans-Atlantic Single Handers' Race of 1968, in which she placed third behind two larger boats.

Cheers might be described as a catamaran, since she has two hulls, but she might also be described as a trimaran with only two hulls. She is 40 feet long, but all her living accommodations are in one hull and all her sail is rigged over the same hull. This hull is always kept to weather, because *Cheers* sails in either direction.

A trimaran sails on only two of its hulls at a time—the main hull plus whichever of the outrigging hulls happens to be to lee. The third hull, the outrigging hull to weather, is simply carried along. It comes into play only when the vessel changes tack and it becomes the lee hull. The opposite outrigging hull then gets carried along, high and dry, until the tack is changed again.

Cheers is similar to a trimaran, but with the weather outrigging hull eliminated. Her one outrigging hull can always be kept to lee because when the crew wants her to go the other direction, they do not turn her around, they just simply stop and then start sailing again in the other direction.

The ancient proas of the Pacific islands had asymmetrical hulls, but unlike modern catamarans, which have the curved sides of the hulls facing each other, the curved sides of the ancient proas both face in the same direction, to weather. However, Newick did not adopt this feature. The hulls of *Cheers* are symmetrical.

Cheers has two masts, which are identical and are set an equal distance from the lengthwise center of the main hull. On each mast is a Marconi sail, and they also are identical. They are rigged in such a manner that they will swing 180 degrees, from straight up and down the main hull in one direction to straight up and down in the other.

To a certain extent *Cheers* can be controlled by dumping one of the sails while leaving the other filled. In combination, the center of effort of the two sails is directly over the center of the boat, but if one sail only is developing power, the center of effort shifts to that sail and a turning moment is introduced. The boat also is controlled by two daggerboards, one more or less at the base of each mast. By varying the depths of the daggerboards, such as pulling one up while leaving the other down, the combined center of lateral resistance can be shifted, which also can be used to introduce a turning moment.

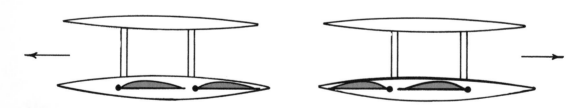

THE PROA. The proa is an ancient design of sailing craft from the Pacific Islands. It has a main hull and a smaller outrigging hull connected by crossbeams, and it is set up to sail in either direction. The sail (or sails) is reversible, and both the main hull and the outrigger are double-ended so that the craft can be sailed forward or backward. In fact, the craft has no forward or backward, as it sails equally well in either direction. The purpose of making the craft sail in either direction is that the outrigging hull can always be kept to lee. To go in reverse, the sail is simply rotated around the mast. Dick Newick, of the U. S. Virgin Islands, designed a craft on these principles that placed third in the 1968 Trans-Atlantic Single-Handers' Race.

Cheers was designed for speed, and she is a fast boat. Her hulls are extremely thin and narrow. Her accommodations are for only one man, and even then they are extremely cramped. The general type could perhaps be scaled up or the hulls otherwise enlarged to provide accommodations for cruising, but as far as we know it has not been tried. Newick designed *Cheers'* control mechanisms specifically so that they could be handled easily by one man and so that the boat could be balanced out and sailed "hands off" for long periods of time. Though it is of little importance in the race she was built for, *Cheers* is difficult in tight maneuvers and modifications would have to be made to rectify this before the design could become widely popular as a cruising type. Even so the problem is unlikely to be difficult.

Even when the proa is modified to a cruising boat, it probably faces an uphill battle for acceptance for no other reason than that it is unconventional. Cruising catamarans, which became a successful design over 25 years ago, even now have not made great inroads with the yachting public, and cruising trimarans, which got an even later start, are also being accepted at a very slow rate. Judging from the prejudices against cats and tris, it will be a decade before cruising proas are seen in any great numbers.

Part of the resistance to trimarans as cruising yachts has come from proponents of catamarans, and trimaran proponents have been known to question the catamaran design. The question of which is the fastest is, at present, unanswerable. Class C, which is the main competitive event for pure speed, is technically a catamaran affair, and most of the vessels entered from year to year have been catamarans. Trimarans have been allowed in the competition, but too few of them have been built and entered for any relative evaluation to be meaningful. Just offhand it would appear that there is little to choose between the two designs from a standpoint of all-out peak speed.

As for other factors, the following can be said for catamarans: they are easier to build; they have less beam and therefore take up less room in harbors; and in general, since they have one less hull, they have less windage and presumably are more weatherly, but this is far from certain.

On the side of trimarans the arguments run: they have a lower center of gravity, because weight is concentrated in the main hull; they can have more comfortable accommodations (for any given size) because of the depth of room in the main hull; they are structurally sounder, because the mast(s) is supported directly on a hull instead of by a bridge between two hulls; and the installation of an auxiliary engine is far less of a problem because the machinery and the fuel cells can be put in the center hull where they will need no counterbalance, as they most certainly do if put in one hull or the other of a catamaran.

Weight distribution, whether in design or in loading, has to be carefully attended to in any multihull. On a monohull that weighs several thousand pounds, 100 pounds here or there has little effect in throwing the hull out of trim. On multihulls, however, which weigh very little, a few pounds carelessly misplaced can cause the boat to ride down on one corner or one side and greatly cut into performance.

Whichever is best, catamarans or trimaran, multihulls in general have some definite advantages over monohulls. They tend to be more comfortable and easier to live on because they have far less roll. And multihulls are irrefutably faster than monohulls.

All-out peak speed is of little importance for cruising multihulls. The high speeds (30 knots or whatever the current claim) of the hot racing machines are never reached except on that rare condition of high winds and low seas, but in a variety of conditions, such as would be met on a long voyage, multihulls can be expected to do from a third to half again better than monohulls of the same length.

Because multihulls are so easily driven, owners of cruising types can exercise the option to under-rig their vessels for the purpose of making sail handling easier, and also for the purpose of saving money.

Highly tuned racing rigs are expensive, both to buy and to maintain, and they are also a lot of work to operate. By using some of the more durable developments in rigging, and by under-rigging, a multihull owner can save considerable amounts of money, and have a rig that is easy to operate while still just as fast, or faster, than a highly tuned monohull.

The only thing to be said against multihulls is the prospect of a capsize, but the danger there is really very small. Few cruising-size multihulls have capsized, and in nearly all those cases the blame could be laid either to carelessness or to recklessness.

X Real Wind and Apparent Wind

High-speed hull designs and high-power rigging have brought about some changes in sailing technique in the past few years. The new techniques have brought about modifications in equipment.

Behind the changes is the greater difference between real wind and apparent wind, which is caused by higher speeds.

For the purpose of this discussion, let us say that there are three kinds of wind: real wind, false wind, and apparent wind.

The real wind is just what the name implies, air moving in the atmosphere, or the wind that everyone is familiar with.

Everyone is also reasonably familiar with false wind. If it is a perfectly calm day, but you are driving north in an automobile at 50 miles per hour and happen to stick your arm out the window, your arm will feel the effect of a northerly wind of 50 miles per hour. The effect is false wind.

Apparent wind is the combined effect of real wind and false wind. Suppose that you are still driving north at 50 miles per hour, but as you do so

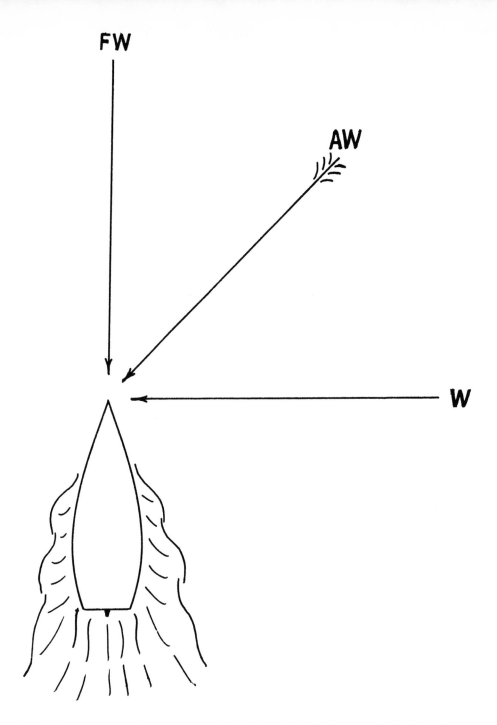

APPARENT WIND. The apparent wind is the wind relative to a boat that is in motion. It is the wind as it appears, in direction and velocity, to the crew of a boat. There are two ingredients to apparent wind, false wind and real wind. In the drawing, assume that the boat is traveling at 25 miles per hour. The boat, by its own motion through the air, is creating a false wind (labeled FW) of 25 miles per hour. Assume that the real wind (labeled W) is blowing 25 miles per hour directly across the course of the boat. In this case, the apparent wind (labeled AW) is halfway between the false wind and the real wind. The apparent wind is always somewhere between the two, and the faster a boat travels, the nearer it will be to the false wind.

a real wind starts blowing from the west at 50 miles per hour. The combined effect of the real wind and the false wind would make it appear that the wind was actually blowing from halfway between north and west and that it was blowing at about 71 miles per hour. This is apparent wind.

On low-speed sailboats, such as conventional, displacement-type yachts or small dinghies, the difference between real wind and apparent wind is not great. Sails have to be adjusted according to the apparent wind rather than the real wind, but this is a small adjustment learned almost unconsciously. A person aboard a boat is confronted only with the apparent wind and rarely even has to think about the difference between apparent and real wind.

For builders and sailors of high-speed sailing boats, however, the difference is of more than academic interest. High-speed sailing boats, especially iceboats but also some experimental soft-water boats of late, are capable, at times, of sailing faster than the speed of the real wind itself. This means that on such boats, the false wind is, at times, greater than the real wind. In other words, the false wind has more to do with determining the direction of apparent wind than does the real wind. This is never the case on a low-speed, conventional boat.

Obviously it is apparent wind that flows across the sails of a moving boat, and since it can differ so widely from real wind on a high-speed boat, allowances have to be made for it. Recently sailors and designers have not only made allowances for it but have actually taken advantage of it to make their fast boats even faster. How this has been done will be explained shortly, but first it is necessary to understand the basic mechanics of Marconi sails.

Modern sails are shaped like airfoils and whenever possible are set so that they deflect the wind about 45 degrees from the direction from which it strikes the sail. The air molecules are forced into a turn, which they negotiate smoothly, but in so turning they take on a centrifugal force. Since the sail is the thing forcing the turn, it is the thing to which the centrifugal force is transferred.

To be efficient, sails must turn the air 45 degrees, give or take 5 degrees. If sails are trimmed to turn the air less than 45 degrees, centrifugal force is reduced and power is lost. At about 30 degrees, the loss is so severe on most rigs that the sail luffs, meaning that it begins to flutter because there is not enough force even to keep the fabric blown out full, let alone enough to drive the boat.

If sails are trimmed to turn the air more than 45 degrees, the air will cease to flow smoothly. It will break up into eddies and the sail will be merely a perpendicular obstruction across the wind, rather than an efficient airfoil.

The Marconi rig is popular, first because it is handy and can be readily shaped into an airfoil, but secondly because it is efficient on four of the five basic points of sailing. Let us take the points one at a time. Imagine a top view of a boat out of the water, and the wind is blowing, throughout this entire example, from north to south.

1. *Beating*. The boat is headed either northwest or northeast. The boom of the Marconi sail is hauled in tight, directly along the center line of the boat, or as near so as possible. Since the boat itself is headed off the wind 45 degrees, the wind is being deflected 45 degrees, so this is an efficient point of sail. The boat cannot head any closer to due north because the sail cannot be hauled in any farther.[1] If the skipper wants to make good a course that is due north, he must zigzag, sailing first northwest and then northeast.

Boats sail against the wind because their lateral resistance keeps them moving on a straight line, just like track keeps a rail car on a straight line. You can cause a toy train car to move along its track by pushing on it almost sideways with your finger. Of course, if you push directly sideways, the car will not roll, but if you turn your finger just a little bit away from perpendicular and push gently, the car will move. Because of the partial vacuum in front of the arch of an airfoil, there is a slight forward element in the thrust. Most of the thrust of a sail is sideways (which is why boats heel so much when they are beating), but it is just a little bit forward, and this is what causes the boat to move along its "track," even against the wind.

2. *Close reach*. The boat's heading is somewhere between northwest and due west, or between northeast and due east. However, the boom has been let out of the center line of the boat somewhat so that it still is on the northwest-southeast line (or, if the other tack, the northeast-southwest line). The boom's position, relative to the wind, has not changed. It is still at a 45-degree angle to the wind, so this also is an efficient point of sail.

3. *Beam reach*. The boat is headed due east or due west. The boom has been let out farther from the center line of the boat, but it remains at the same 45-degree angle relative to the wind, and so is still working like an airfoil.

4. *Broad reach*. The boat is headed between west and southwest or between east and southeast, but the boom has been let out even farther and is still remaining at a 45-degree angle to the wind. If the boat is headed

---

[1]Some boats can effectively sail closer than this to the wind, but for the ordinary boat with ordinary rigging, 45-degrees off is about the practical limit. Though the average boat will continue to move when pointed up to 35 or even 30 degrees, so much speed is being lost that the savings in distance does not compensate for it.

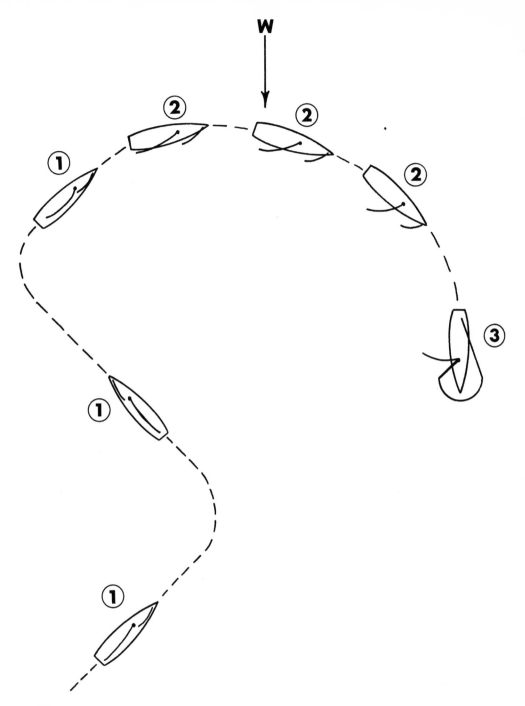

POINTS OF SAILING. *For the ordinary sailboat, the basic points of sailing are beating (1), where the boat is zigzagging to make a course against the wind; reaching (2), where the wind is more or less at the side of the vessel; and running (3), where the boat is traveling in the same direction the wind is blowing. On conventional sailboats, an extra sail, the spinnaker, is often used for running, but even so the speed of the boat is limited to the speed at which the wind is blowing. Some experimental high-speed boats of the last few years have been able to run downwind faster than the speed at which the wind is blowing.*

due southwest or due southeast the boom will be straight out to the side of the boat. In this position it will be against the shrouds, so that it cannot be swung out any farther; however, this is still an efficient point of sail.

5. *Running*. The boat's heading is somewhere between southwest and southeast, but because the shrouds are in the way of the boom, it is no longer at a 45-degree angle to the wind. On this point of sailing, the Marconi sail ceases to be an airfoil and instead becomes a perpendicular obstruction to the wind, just like a square sail.

The limitation is strictly a mechanical problem in the rigging and has nothing to do with aerodynamics. If it were possible for the sail to swing on around until it could be trimmed at a 45-degree angle to a following wind, the sail could develop much more power. In fact, a few very small boats that have free-standing masts (masts without shrouds or stays) can actually be sailed running with the boom out over the bow on one side or the other.

Such an arrangement on larger boats is impractical, however, because it creates more problems than it solves. For one thing, a free-standing mast has to be heavily constructed and results in a lot of weight aloft. If this weight is counterbalanced by ballast, all-up weight (displacement) is increased, and so, then, is wetted surface. All this slows the boat on all other points of sailing simply for a gain in efficiency in running, and it simply is not worth it. On a very small boat, however, where the persons aboard constitutes a high percentage of the total weight, their bodies are adequate ballast for a rather heavy mast.

The spinnaker is used to make up for the deficiency in power caused by the mainsail operating inefficiently as a perpendicular obstruction. The spinnaker itself is also a rather inefficient sail; it is simply a means of adding to the area of the obstruction. Some sloops are sailed without spinnakers and for running the mainsail is let out over one side of the boat and the jib "winged out" over the other side with a thin pole that is fastened on one end of the jib clew and on the other end to the mast.

For a boat to use a spinnaker, it is necessary that it have a backstay. The spinnaker exerts considerable pressure on the mast in a forward direction, and a mast would have to be very heavy to stand it without backstaying.

In the days before 1910, when the Marconi sail evolved, boats with spinnakers had to use running backstays. The problem was that standing backstays (backstays permanently attached at the masthead and at the center of the stern) would be in the way of the gaff and prevent it from swinging from side to side. The solution was to use two backstays, attached together somewhere up on the mast (not necessarily at the head) and running from there to the rails somewhere aft. The endings of these stays at the rail were on release mechanisms so that the lee backstay could be slackened to prevent it from impeding the swing of the boom, gaff, and sail. These stays are called "running" because they can be slackened and tightened, not because they are used on the running point of sail.

Some Marconi-rigged boats today have running backstays, and the usual reason is that it has such a large reach that a standing backstay would be in its way. However, such rigging is usually found only on racing boats. Running backstays are bothersome. One has to be tightened and the other slackened just as the boat is changing tack, which is one of the busiest moments in operation of a sailboat even without having to change stays. Some of the boats do not have backstays of either kind.

Apparent wind is always forward of the real wind. When a boat is under-way, the wind will appear to be coming at the boat over a point nearer to the bow than the real wind. Another way of looking at it is that the false wind always comes at the boat from dead ahead, right straight over the bow and along the center line of the hull. The apparent wind, then, is always somewhere between the false wind and the real wind.

How far forward the apparent wind is from the real wind depends on the relative speeds of the real wind and the false wind. The faster the false wind, the farther forward the apparent wind will be. In other words, the faster a boat is moving, the farther forward the apparent wind will be.

High-speed boats, when they get going, are almost always operating in apparent wind that is well up toward the bow. That is why iceboats, which can travel five or six times real-wind speed, always have sails close-hauled. Suppose an iceboat is sailing southwest in a real wind that is blowing from north to south. The speed of the boat will be so great that the wind will appear to be blowing from the west, or even from west-southwest.

Now an ordinary, low-speed boat sailing southwest in a northerly wind would be on a broad reach, and its sail would be let all of the way out until the boom touched the shrouds. But a high-speed boat traveling in the same direction cannqt sail in this way. As the boat speed picks up, the wind appears to shift more and more around to the west, and for the sail to be kept at about a 45-degree angle of attack, it has to be hauled in more and more. The more the sail is hauled in, the faster the boat goes, and the faster the boat goes, the more the sail has to be hauled in, until finally the sail is actually trimmed at close-hauled position, even though the boat, with respect to the real wind, is on a broad reach.

Iceboats can sail so much faster close-hauled on a broad reach that they never sail directly in the direction the wind is blowing. In other words, iceboats are never on the point of sail called running. Even though the dis-

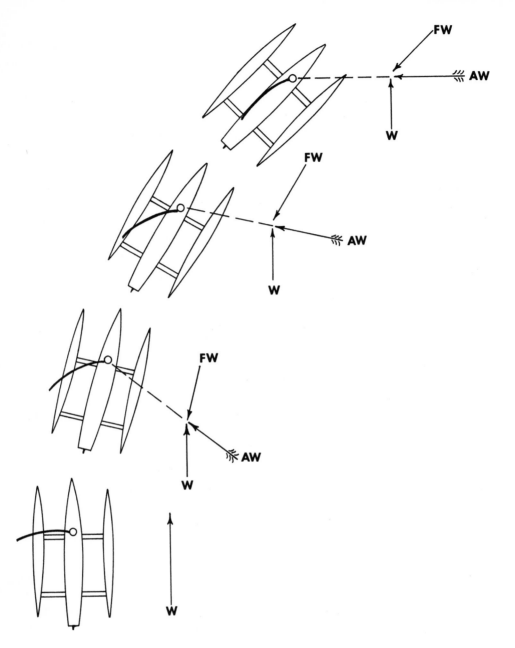

ACCELERATION. Modern high-speed multihulls and iceboats sail with the wind faster than the speed at which the wind is blowing. The trick is to use the speed of the boat itself to bring the apparent wind (AW) farther and farther toward the bow so that the boat can sail close-hauled. At the bottom of the drawing, the trimaran is starting up from a dead stop. Its sail is winged out and is forming a perpendicular obstruction to the wind. In the second drawing, the boat is starting to gain speed and the false wind (FW) is beginning to bring the apparent wind around to the side, making it necessary to start hauling in the sail. In the third drawing, the trimaran has gained more speed, bringing the apparent wind more to the side. At the same time the craft heads more into the apparent wind and the sail is hauled even closer. In the top drawing the boat has accelerated to the point that the apparent wind is at a right angle to the real wind (W). The boat has turned in to meet the apparent wind at a 45-degree angle. At this point the sail is close-hauled.

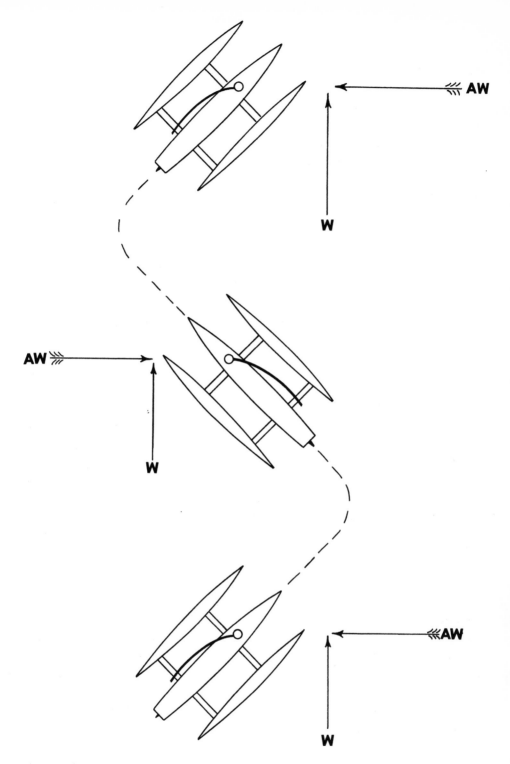

TACKING DOWNWIND. By accelerating to the point that the apparent wind is at right angles to the real wind, a modern racing trimaran or catamaran can zigzag, close-hauled, downwind. The distance covered in zigzagging is about one-third longer than the same distance in a straight line, so a boat only has to go more than a third again faster to gain from tacking. Modern racing multihulls can go two to three times as fast tacking downwind as they can running dead downwind. Iceboats can go about six times the speed of the wind.

tance is one-third farther, they can make much faster time to a mark dead downwind by zigzagging (tacking down wind), close-hauled on one broad reach and then on the other.

Since iceboats never run, they never carry spinnakers. No sailing vessel, whether it be an iceboat, a soft-water boat, or a land yacht, can sail faster than the speed of the real wind when it is moving in line with the real wind. In fact the speed of the real wind is the theoretical maximum speed of a boat that is running. In practice the boats sail less than the speed of the real wind. A spinnaker can help the boat get up closer to the theoretical maximum, but neither it nor anything else yet invented can make it go beyond.

The possibility that spinnakers may become extinct is raised by recent trends in International Catamaran Development Class C, the foremost experimental sailing class for multihulls.

Meade Gougeon, one of the authors of this book, has at the age of thirty-four had twenty-five years' experience in building and sailing both iceboats and soft-water boats. He decided in the middle 1960's to try to adapt the iceboat technique of downwind tacking to soft-water boats. He chose the trimaran design concept as the vehicle for his experiments, and he built four of them, each an improvement on the one preceding. The idea began showing promise in 1966 when Gougeon used the third one of his trimarans tacking downwind to build up tremendous leads over the field on downwind legs of the One-of-a-Kind regatta at Miami, Florida, beating the second-place boat, a much larger Class A scow, by nearly an hour in a four-hour race. His boat was disqualified from that race for touching a mark, and in a later race some gear on the machine broke down and the boat had to be withdrawn from the series.

Gougeon perfected downwind tacking in 1969 with his fourth trimaran, *Victor T*, which won the North American Multihull Championship that summer at Hamilton, Ontario. At the One-of-a-Kind regatta at Chicago that fall he posted the fastest time around a set of marks ever recorded in the second race before having to quit the series because of structural failure. He had proved his point, however, and tacking downwind has since become a universal technique in Class C racing.

While tacking downwind holds promise, it is not something that can yet be adapted to cruising boats, especially small ones, in the immediate future. The requirements are first of all an extremely lightweight boat (*Victor T*, Gougeon's trimaran of 1969, is 25 feet long and 18 feet across the beam, yet weighs just over 300 pounds). To tack downwind the boat must be light and otherwise capable of very high speed, for high speed is the only thing that can make the apparent wind swing forward to the point that the boat can be sailed close-hauled on beam reach. It is improbable that any monohull vessel, unless it were several hundred feet long, could ever be made to tack downwind. The hull speed of a large vessel might make it theoretically possible, but the problem of scaling up Marconi rigging to such proportions renders such a thing unlikely. Big multihulls, if they were built lightly and were not loaded so heavily, quite possibly could take advantage of the development, and in fact it has been done with a 35-foot trimaran of limited accommodations for four. The boat is *Adagio*, which was built and launched in 1970 at the Gougeon Brothers factory in Bay City, Michigan.

XI Hydrofoils

Strictly speaking, any part of a boat that moves beneath the water, with the purpose of creating a force, is a hydrofoil. This would include centerboards and fins, which create a force to counter leeway; the entire underbody of hulls, which to a certain extent do the same thing; and rudders, which create a force that can be controlled and by which hulls are maneuvered.

All of the above are examples of hydrofoils that generate force horizontally. Hydrofoils also can be used to generate vertical forces for a variety of purposes, such as stabilizing hulls. Most commonly, though, hydrofoils are thought of as devices that lift entire hulls out of the water and fly them along at high speeds just above the surface. Foil-borne motorboats are now common, and many sailing machines have gotten up and attained high speeds on foils.

Hydrofoils are devices that operate *in* the water, not on top of it. A water ski is not a hydrofoil. The most efficient hydrofoils (those that generate the most power) are arched on one side, flat on the other, similar to the shape of an airfoil. At optimum performance, arched hydrofoils develop low pressure in the water passing around the arch, which reduces the foil's resistance to rising, allowing the pressure on the flat side to push the foil upward more easily.

Motorized boats were first made to ride up on hydrofoils, completely clear of the water, before the turn of this century. An Italian named Forlanini had a rather large boat, apparently 50 or 60 feet in length, up on foils in 1898. The Wright brothers, credited with the first powered flight of an airplane, experimented with a hydrofoil boat before 1910, and in 1918, Alexander Graham Bell, better known for his invention of the telephone, had built an 11,000-pound air boat (powered by two Liberty aircraft engines of 350 horsepower each) that rose on hydrofoils and traveled at 60 miles per hour.

Today, large and small hydrofoil power boats are fairly common and very successful. Speeds of 50 and 60 knots on foil-borne ferries, large enough to carry a dozen or so automobiles and hundreds of passengers, are common in Europe. The largest foil-borne vessel is the U. S. Navy's *Plainview*, an experimental vessel 212 feet long and weighing 320 tons. It was built in Seattle, Washington, by Lockheed Shipbuilding & Construction Co., and delivered to the Navy in the summer of 1969.

The most common system of hydrofoils, whether for powerboats or sailboats, is to mount two foils, one on each side of the hull just ahead of the center of gravity, and a third foil in the center of the hull at the stern. The two forward foils bear about 90 percent of the weight, and the stern foil is used to steer. Some variations are two foils near the center of gravity and one out on the bow; four foils, two near the bow and two near the stern; and four foils, two in the middle of the hull and one each at the bow and the stern.

Whatever the system in which they are mounted, there are two basic types of the foils, self-stabilizing and adjustable. Self-stabilizing foils are fixed and their angle of attack on the water through which they pass cannot be changed. On the adjustable type, the angle of the foil is controlled.

Self-stabilizing foils are either the V type or the ladder type. Ladder-type foils are actually several foils, parallel and in a vertical row, like rungs on a ladder. They are held in place by vertical stringers, just the way a ladder is built, or by a single stringer in the center. The purpose of the design is that as a boat moves through the water, the pressure on the foils causes the "ladder" to rise, lifting the hull. As the boat speed increases the additional pressure will cause the top foils (rungs) to rise out of the water. As individual foils, one by one, come out, the lift of the total assembly is reduced. If there were six foils on the ladder, then when the top foil

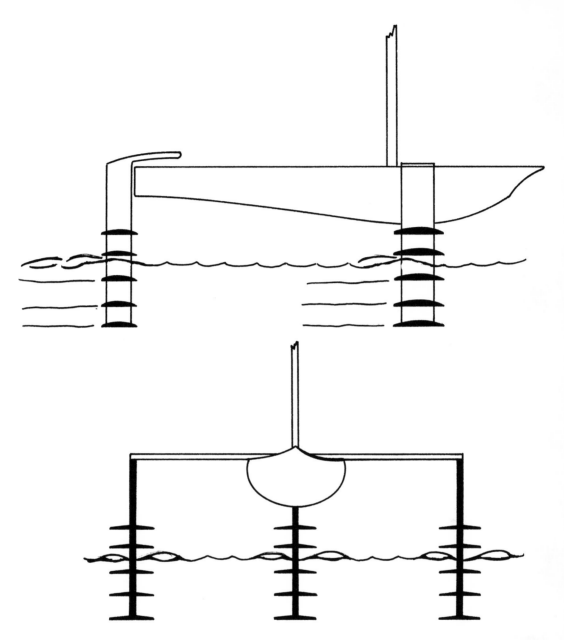

LADDER-TYPE FOILS. The oldest system of hydrofoils used to fly hulls above the water is the ladder type. A ladder foil is actually several foils, the shape of little airplane wings, mounted on a vertical strut. Three such struts of these foils are usually used, as in the illustration. Ladder-type foils were first used on motorboats around the turn of the century and adapted to sailboats, with limited success, after World War II. The system is self-stabilizing, because as the boat accelerates the ladders lift themselves out of the water, step by step. As a step lifts out, the lift of the ladder as a whole is proportionately reduced so that at any given speed, the ladder will ride at a certain level. In the illustration, the drawings show the boat flying with two foils above water on all three struts. If wind or wave forces one side of the boat down, an extra foil on the strut on that side is forced into the water. The foil immediately causes extra lift on that side, which brings the boat back level.

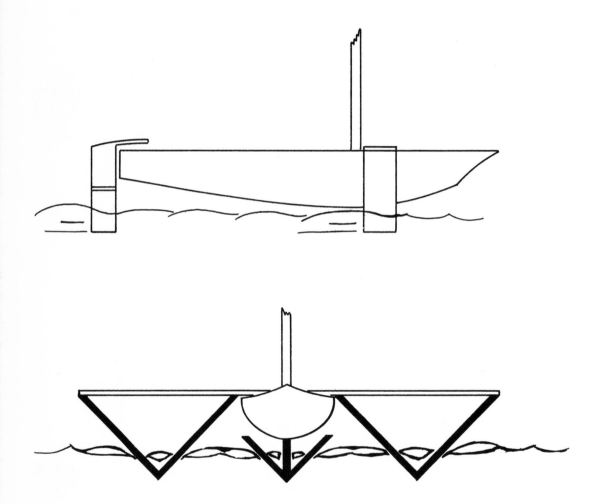

V FOILS. V foils, like ladder foils, are self-stabilizing. As the boat gains speed, the V rides higher and higher in the water, leaving less and less foil area down in the water, and therefore reducing lift. At any given speed the foils will stabilize and ride at a certain level. If one side of the boat is forced down, the foil on that side will instantly develop more lift, which will bring the craft back to level. The trouble with V foils is that they are very inefficient. Since the foil surfaces are set at an angle, part of the energy they generate is to the side. Though this sidethrust is in two different directions and therefore is self-canceling, it nonetheless creates a great deal of drag, the only countermeasure to which is extra power.

was forced out of the water, the lift would be reduced by one-sixth, when the second foil came above the surface, the lift would be reduced by one-third, and so on. Thus the more the foil assembly lifts, the less it is capable of lifting, so that at any given speed the foil rides at a level of equilibrium. This is what is meant by the term "self-stabilizing."

One might say that a V foil is actually two foils connected in the form of a V. In operation, the bottom of the V is down. When most of the V is submerged, a lot of the area of the foils is under water. As the foil rises, however, the area beneath the water is steadily reduced, and as this foil area is reduced, so is the foil's capacity to lift. The result is exactly the same as with the ladder foil in that at any given speed a level of equilibrium is established.

The third type of foil assembly, the T foil, is not self-stabilizing. The assembly is the shape of an upside-down letter T. The crossbar of the T is the foil, and the rest of the letter is a strut that connects the foil to the hull. To keep T foils running at a constant depth, it is necessary that their angle of attack be adjustable, something like an aileron or an elevator on an airplane.

The T configuration is the most efficient foil assembly. It gives the most lift for the least amount of drag. Ladder foils have a great deal of wetted surface because their lifting area is broken up into so many segments. The extra wetted surface causes a lot of drag. V foils also have a lot of drag, but for a different reason. They can use only half the lift they produce because the lift is at an angle.

While hydrofoils have been very successfully applied to power boats, they have not shown much promise under sail. This could change, of course, but there are some formidable problems to overcome. The main one is the fluctuation of power (and therefore, speed) because of changes in wind velocity.

A power boat can be designed and engines installed so that the vessel can travel steadily within a very predictable range of speed. Foils can be designed to operate efficiently within this speed because there are assurances that the speed can be steadily maintained. The problems in designing hydrofoils are similar to those of designing airplane wings. Foils that are large in area and have a lot of arch in the top surface will lift a boat out of the water at low speeds, but they develop a lot of drag that prevents the craft they are supporting from traveling at high speed. Foils that are small in area and have a low arch develop less drag and permit high speeds, but then they do not have much lift at low speeds.

The speed of sailboats, in spite of all the advances in rigging in the past few years, is still a close function of the speed at which the wind is blowing. Thus far there has been little success in developing a system of foils

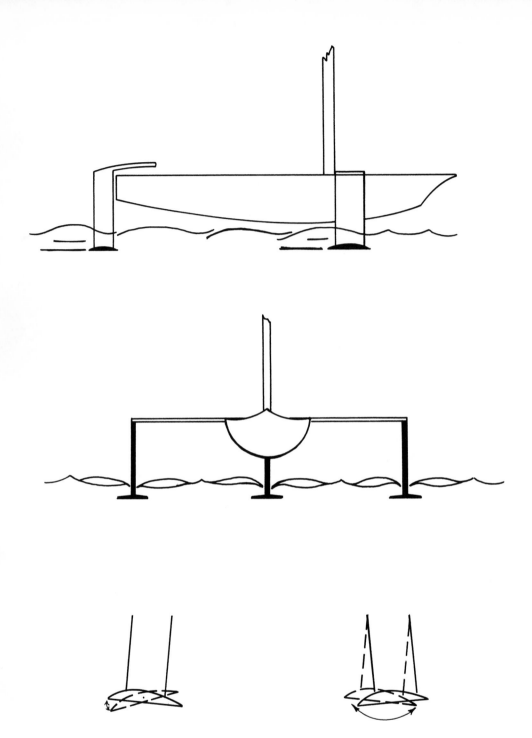

T FOILS. T foils have the least amount of wetted surface for the amount of lift they generate and are therefore the most efficient of hydrofoil systems. They are not, however, self-stabilizing, so means must be provided to control the lift of each individual foil. The usual method is to control lift by changing the foils' angles of attack, as in the two bottom drawings. T foils are currently favored on large hydrofoil power boats where the attitudes of the foils are controlled automatically by power machinery linked to leveling sensors. There have been experiments with this type of foil on sailing craft with attitudes controlled either manually or by mechanical linkages to floats.

that will operate over a wide enough range to be very useful on a sailing craft.

Another problem with hydrofoil boats—and it is a problem of power boats and sailboats alike—is that they do not operate well in high waves, waves that are tall enough to touch the hull. In low, choppy seas where the foils lift the boat above the peaks, foil boats function marvelously, giving a much smoother ride at much higher speeds than is possible with a conventional hull. However, when the chop gets high enough so that the peaks are lapping at the hull, the boat is slowed, and it has to get down in the water and plow through just like a conventional hull. Of course, the larger the boat, the bigger the chop it can clear.

On high waves of long frequency, where boats have to climb and descend peaks and valleys, such as is the usual condition out in the oceans, few hydrofoil craft will operate, because the foils will not raise the craft on the front of a wave or let it down on the wave's back. The only solution to this problem, so far, is a system by which the foil angle of attack can be controlled to raise the craft going up a wave and pull it down as it descends a wave. Systems of manual control for this purpose have been tried, but they have proved to be so difficult and tedious to operate that the system is unreliable. Large motorized hydrofoil boats have an advantage in this area because they are capable of carrying power equipment, activated by sensors, to manipulate automatically the angles of incidence of the foils. Such elaborate equipment, which cannot practically be used on sailing vessels, keeps the bottom of the hull at a constant distance above the surface. On smaller boats, floats that skim along in front of the hull, connected in direct mechanical linkage to control angle of incidence, have been tried, but none has yet proved satisfactory.

There were some hydrofoil sailing machines before World War II, but the first experimenter in this field to draw much attention was Gordon Baker of Evansville, Wisconsin. In the early 1950's, Baker built several machines, some with V foils, some with ladder-type foils, and some with a combination of the two, and succeeded in getting a contract from the U. S. Navy to carry on his experiments. Like iceboats and the latest Class C catamarans, Baker's hydrofoils easily sailed faster than the wind that propelled them.

Dozens, or even hundreds, of experimenters have followed Baker in trying to come up with a hydrofoil machine that would operate in a wide variety of conditions. Many different foil systems and designs have been tried, but none has yet worked well enough to suggest even remotely that hydrofoils are a viable concept for a cruising type of sailing yacht.

It would appear—and it may turn out that way yet—that iceboat-type rigging and sailing technique, which gets a tremendous amount of power out of a small amount of wind, would be able to drive hydrofoil craft at consistently high speeds and thus overcome the problem that foils cannot be designed to work at low speed as well as high speed. However, there are two problems that experimenters keep running into.

First, while hydrofoil craft have less resistance than other types of soft-water boats, they nonetheless have far greater resistance than do iceboats. While iceboats sail five to six times wind speed, the best sailing hydrofoils have done so far is possibly two times wind speed, and there is little reason to think they will ever do a lot better.

Second, while it is true that iceboat rigs and techniques develop tremendous amounts of power at high speeds, they develop very little power at low speeds. Unless the wind is blowing 15 or 20 miles per hour, iceboats have to be pushed off by hand to get them going. Once they get going and the rig starts to draw, the iceboat becomes a very powerful machine, but at low speeds it is very helpless.

Hydrofoil craft need a great deal of power in the low speed range because they encounter their greatest resistance when their hulls are down in the water and they are trying to get up on their foils. Since hydrofoil sailing boats cannot be pushed off, the alternative is to tow them with a motorboat until they get up on their foils and get going. All the really fast hydrofoil sailing boats (20 miles per hour and up) around to date require this kind of sendoff. Many other hydrofoil sailing craft are capable of getting up by themselves, but all of them have rather large, high-arched foils and therefore are incapable of speeds beyond 10 to 15 miles per hour.

In other words, with the current state of the art, sailing hydrofoil craft can either sail at high speeds or they can get up by themselves, but they cannot do both.

XII Modern Keelboats ...and Some Speculation

Scientific knowledge, new materials, and new skills, which have brought fast iceboats, planing dinghies, catamarans, and trimarans, also have brought big improvements in large keelboats.

The large keelboats of today, whether they are fitted out for ocean racing or are just family cruisers, are a lot better and a lot less expensive than they were just a few years ago. They are not as good as they could be—or we should say they are not as good as they will be in a few years—but most of today's keelboats are nonetheless the best ever built.

Plastic hulls, which became a big thing starting about 1960, have revolutionized the keelboat business. For one thing, they cost about half as much as hulls framed up and planked in wood. The price of a total, fitted-out boat of plastic is about a third less than it was a few years ago.

The plastic hulls have larger accommodations than planked wooden hulls of the same size outside. The plastic is thinner than planking and there are no bulky frames inside as there must be for a planked hull.

From a standpoint of performance, boats of modern materials are better because they weigh less. Hulls, decks, and cabins of plastic and spars of aluminum are lighter than comparable items in conventional construction of wood. And none of the modern materials will soak up water, which is an additional saving in weight.

Boats of modern materials, being lighter all over, need less ballast on the bottom to keep them upright. All-up weight is less; less power is needed to drive at hull speed, and therefore it has been possible to reduce sail area. It also has been possible to reduce sail area because changes in rigging have made sails more powerful for their size. One of the biggest improvements in rigging in recent years is the masthead jib. Formerly jibs were not as tall as the mainsail, but the modern style, which is much more efficient, is for the jib as well as the mainsail to run all the way to the head of the mast. Masthead jibs that overlap the mainsail (Genoa jibs) are extremely powerful and produce perhaps as much as 75 percent of the total power of the jib and main together. Reductions in sail area plus modern, efficient hardware for sail handling has taken a lot of work out of yachting.

Light as modern keelboats are, the technology is available to make them even lighter. Builders of the ultralightweight multihulls for the experimental classes are returning to wood as their construction material. Wood and epoxy glues, when used together and properly engineered, make a far stronger construction at far less weight than plastic.

Over the past several years Gougeon Brothers have worked up a system of construction in which they saturate all wooden parts in epoxy. The saturation has shown three clear advantages. First, the epoxy increases the strength of the wood in compression. Second, since the epoxy forms a sealed encasement around the wood, it locks moisture in the wood at a permanent level. Since the wood can neither take on nor expel moisture, it cannot swell or shrink. In short, it makes wood a very stable material for engineering. Third, the same seal locks air out of the wood grain and makes the wood impervious to rot.

There also is an economic benefit to epoxy saturation. Because the epoxy bolsters the strength, inexpensive wood can be used in construction without any adverse effects.

Gougeon Brothers use the epoxy saturation to build iceboats, multihulls, and monohulls, applying it to conventional construction, cold-molded plywood construction, or sheet plywood construction, turning out hulls that weigh far less than comparable boats in plastic. Most builders in the experimental classes, several custom yacht builders, and many amateurs are adopting the technique, which could, and probably will, spread through the field of keelboats in the next few years. It might have done so already except for two things: most of the current rating rules heavily penalize light displacement, and molded plywood construction, the chief rival to plastic in strength and weight, lends itself more to custom building (or patient amateur building) than to mass production.

Another promising construction, but one that is extremely difficult and expensive, is welded aluminum. In hulls of about 40 feet and over aluminum construction can be lighter and at least as strong as plastic. Only a few yards in the world are capable of welding up yachts in aluminum. The technique is well out of the reach of amateurs because of the difficulty of accurately forming parts and the further complication that the welding, unless done very knowingly, induces distortion in the metal.

The rigging of today's keelboats, as good as it is, could be made more efficient by the use of full-length battens and rotating masts. Higher efficiency would mean less sail area and rigs that are easier to handle. Both have been used successfully on large multihulls. A few large oceangoing catamarans and trimarans that have rotating masts set them up to carry spinnakers.

With improvements in lightweight construction, keelboats may look quite a bit different in a few years. The keelboats of the future will be just as fast or faster than the present style, but they will be easier to handle and, because they are light, they probably will ride up over waves instead of plowing through them.

Appearance alone has a lot to do with what is fashionable in sailing yachts, and what is fashionable is the biggest factor in what the rules permit and what the rules do not. Full-length battens and rotating masts are not now fashionable, and at present nearly all racing rules flatly prohibit both.

Another problem with the rules is that many boats, in fact most boats to some extent, are designed to rate well, sometimes at the expense of good cruising qualities. In short, boats, as they are built, are applied to the rule instead of the rule being applied to the boat, and there is no solution in sight for that problem.

But perhaps we should not deplore racing rules so completely—for it is thanks to racing that sailboats have become so sophisticated, and efforts to improve the practical performance of craft within the rules have led to many advances in theory. We now have the technology to make quite fantastic uses of this theory, and perhaps it would be entertaining to close this book with some speculation on such uses and why they might be desirable.

No living person can remember when fossil fuels—coal, petroleum oil, natural gas—were expensive. The fuels have been around in such abundance for so many generations that most of us take their existence for granted.

There was a time, however—and it wasn't all that long ago—when wood, animal fat, and vegetable fat were the main fuels of the world. Candles were made of tallow, lamps burned whale oil or olive oil, and the boilers of steam engines were fired with wood. And only a few years before that, the world depended solely on wind, water, and muscle for mechanical power.

The industrial revolution has, to this date, been a product compounded from two basic elements: the knowledge and the skills to build sophisticated machinery; and the discovery and the exploitation of inexpensive fuels to run the machinery.

The first element is with us to stay. Barring another Dark Age, there is hardly any way in which accumulated knowledge and skills can be depleted. But the second element is certainly subject to depletion.

Of course, the world will not abruptly run out of coal, oil, and natural gas. What will happen is that the easily accessible sources of these fossil fuels will be exhausted and that the world will have to mine coal and drill for oil and gas under more and more difficult circumstances. The inevitable result is that these fuels will become more and more expensive. In fact, in the more highly developed regions of the world this trend is already apparent. As fossil fuels become ever more expensive, there will come a time when other types of energy are cheaper, as was the case before the technologies of mining and drilling were well known.

Nuclear power may become competitive as the price of fossil fuels goes up, but it may not. There is the problem of disposing of radioactive waste. The solution to that right now is to bury it deep in the ground, but this is obviously only a temporary solution. As nuclear power stations increase in number, a more satisfactory solution to disposing of their waste must be found, and the expense of this solution will be the key as to how soon, if at all, nuclear energy becomes competitive in cost with fossil-fuel energy.

Practically all the motor vessels in the world today are powered by fossil fuels. A few military ships (aircraft carriers and submarines) have nuclear power plants, but not because they are cheaper—rather because they are capable of extremely long range without refueling and, in the case of submarines, because they require no oxygen. No commercial ship is currently operating with a nuclear power plant.

The possibility that sails may again be used to power commercial vessels may seem remote. But perhaps it's not quite as farfetched as it seems at first glance. All that is needed is for fossil fuels to increase in price to the point that sailing would be cheaper.

Of course, a return to sail power would not mean a return to anything like the clipper ship. With all of the advances in aerodynamics, hull construction, and sail handling, any sailing ship built today would certainly look a lot different than a clipper. A modern commercial sailing ship would undoubtedly have a fuel-fired generator for shipboard electricity, and a computer linked to power winches which would automatically set and trim sails along with a myriad of push-button controls. It would be a deep-hulled, large-capacity vessel, but of ultralight and ultrastrong construction. When and if we need it, we could build it.

Wind power may also be harnessed in the future for other applications, such as generating electricity. With the modern knowledge and skill for building machines it would certainly be possible to build windmills of great power and reliability, and "pumped storage" could overcome the problem of intermittent wind. In other words, the mills would be used to generate electricity indirectly, by pumping water into an elevated storage basin from which it could be steadily discharged through hydroelectric turbines.

Though these speculations may appear idle, they are by no means beyond the realm of possibility, for wind is a universally abundant, nonpolluting source of energy, a latent source of untold millions of horsepower roaming free in every part of the world. Sailors were the first to recognize and exploit this marvelous natural resource. Perhaps they will not be the last.

Suggested Reading

As was explained in the Introduction, there is something of a shortage of books for the general reader on sailboat design. However, most of the specialized sailing magazines keep well abreast of developments in their chosen areas, and they can be a continuing source of edification for the enthusiast who has read this book with attention. Also, there are a few books that are of considerable value to the reader who wants to learn more about specific subjects.

An excellent book on sailing ships from prehistoric times to the end of the commercial sailing is *The Ship*, by Bjorn Landstrom, published by Doubleday. Landstrom, a Swedish scholar and artist, has filled this volume with hundreds of drawings and paintings, many of them in full color, which trace the appearance of ships.

Many of Landstrom's reconstructions of ancient boats, as he himself repeatedly warns, are highly conjectural. Only half a dozen ships plus some pieces of ships more than a few hundred years old still exist today, and as plans for shipbuilding are a comparatively new thing, the only source materials for pre-Renaissance ships are carvings, paintings, and literature. Landstrom's drawings of later ships become less and less speculative, and those of these last three or four hundred years are undoubtedly quite accurate in detail.

The text of Landstrom's work lacks clear explanation of the ways in which the various rigs were handled by the crews, and offers no comparisons of the aerodynamic efficiency of the rigs. However, the drawings are so well detailed that those with some knowledge of the principles of sailing and aerodynamics will be able to work out reasonable conclusions.

Several books by Howard I. Chapelle, an American, detail the design and construction of American sailing vessels. Among the titles are *The Search for Speed Under Sail, 1700–1855; The History of the American Sailing Ship;* and *American Small Sailing Craft.* All are published by W. W. Norton.

Since sailing developed as a sport, hundreds of books have been published on particular boats, classes of boats, or some specific aspect of sailing. For anyone interested in power and efficiency we recommend *Yacht Racing: The Aerodynamics of Sail,* by Dr. Manfred Curry.

Though Curry's book was first published in 1925, it has been revised since, and the section on aerodynamics contains a wealth of information on how sails work and what makes them work better. In spite of the publication date, most of the information is still valid. The book is still in print, and is published by Scribner in the United States.

Up-to-date information on developments in sailing is catalogued and bound into paperback volumes according to subjects by the Amateur Yacht Research Society (AYRS) of Hermitage, Newbury, Berkshire, England. The AYRS was formed in 1954, and its publications, which include hundreds of articles, drawings, and photographs contributed from all over the world, are edited by Dr. John Morwood, the AYRS founder. In addition to experiments in sailing that have worked, Morwood also documents many failures—things that have been tried and have not worked. A few representative titles are: *Multihull Design & Catamarans; Multihull Seamanship & Trimarans; Foils, Ice Yachts & Sails; Retirement Yachts and Polars;* and *Practical Hydrofoils.* There are dozens of others of very limited scope, such as: *The Wishbone Rig; Fibreglass; Yacht Wind Tunnels;* and *Sail Trimming, Testing & Theory.*

At last count the AYRS had 74 publications available in all, most of them covering contemporary subjects, but a few of them of historical nature.

Index

Aarel, Archie, 84

acceleration of multihulls and iceboats, *illus. 158*

Adagio (trimaran), 161

aerodynamics applied to sail design, 31, 71, 95

A-frame for mast, 80

aft-bending mast, 115, 118, 119; *illus. 116*

air obstruction versus air slice, 91-95; *illus. 93*

airfoil shape, 66, 95, 99, 105, 108, 110, 123, 141, 153, 154, 164; *illus. 111*
in relation to air speed, 112-13 *and n.*
creating, in sails, 113

air flow at varying speeds, 110-13; *illus. 111*

all-up weight, 25, 26, 156, 172

aluminum, 53, 66, 101, 172

Amaryllis (catamaran), 131, 133

America (schooner yacht), 33, 43-44

America's Cup defenders, 28, 30, 39, 44, 45, 47, 52, 126

angle of heel, 33n., 39, 42, 45, 58; *illus. 40, 128*

apparent wind, 105n., 150-53, 157; *illus. 152*

Arab shipping, 13; *illus. 12*

artemon, 7-9, 11; *illus. 8*

aspect ratio, 95n., 102, 108

assymetrical hulls, 141-43, 147; *illus. 136, 142*

Atlantic (3-masted centerboard schooner), 47

atmospheric pressure, 90-91

backstay, standing, *illus. 63*
running, 156-57

Baker, Gordon, 169

balanced helm, 3n., 4-5 *and n.,* 9

ballasting, importance of, 24, 26, 38, 44n., 68, 94, 127, 137, 156, 172; *illus. 41*
outside, 38-39, 45, 56
shifting, 55, 56
in multihull vessels, 130, 135

bark, *illus. 29*

barkentine, *illus. 29*

battens, 97, 99, 108, 113, 122, 124, 173
transverse (full-length), 97-98, 103-5

beam, 33 *and n., 44n.,* 137

beam reach, 133, 154

beating (against the wind), 25, 26, 68, 112, 154; *illus. 155*

Beau Skeeter (iceboat), 82, 84

Beauvais, Walter, 82

bending masts, 115

Bentham, Samuel, 39

Beowulf (catamaran), 133

bilgeboards, 58, 131

bilges, 37-38, 132
hard or rounded, 42

bolt rope, 122

booms, functions of, 9, 21, 30, 61, 102, 108, 112, 113, 119, 154
sideways-bending, 123-24
down-bending, 123n.
eliminating, 124

Booth, Oliver, 76

bottom batten inhaul-outhaul, *illus. 125*

bowlines, 17, 92

bowsprit, 30

bow-steering iceboats, 82-87, 99; *illus. 85, 86*

bow wave, 30n.

box spars, 66; *illus. 107*

bracing, external, 5, 61, 63; *illus. 6, 9, 62*

brails, 5, 9; *illus. 6*

brakes for boats, 98

broad reach (wind on quarter), 112, 154-56

Brown, Woody, 141-42

Buckhout, Jacob E. and George, 78

buckling of mast, 63

buoyancy, center of, 32, 35, 56, 130; *illus. 40, 128*

Burgess, Edward, 39, 44, 45, 52, 94

canoes, 37, 38, 42, 134
double, 13, 17, 130
leeboards on, 35
outrigger, 130, 132

capsizing, dangers of, 45n., 84, 130, 137, 139-40, 145, 150

capstans, 39

caravels, 7, 15, 25; *illus. 16*

catamarans, 30n., 102-3, 108, 127, 130-32, 149, 169, 171, 173; *illus. 128*

cedar for ship timbers, 7

centerboard well, *illus. 37*

centerboards, 5n., 33-35, 52, 58, 131, 141, 143, 163; *illus. 34*
retractable, 44n.; *illus. 46*
hydrofoil (streamlined-shape), 98

Cheers (proa), 147-49

Chesapeake Bay log canoe, 56

China, shipping of, 7, 15, 19; *illus. 20*

Clarel (lateen-rigged iceboat), 80, 82; *illus. 83*

claw sail, 13

clews, 113, 122, 124

clipper ships, 17, 19, 30, 53, 89, 174

closed-course races, 30-31

close-hauled sails, 157; *illus. 158*

close reach, 154

cog, 15, 25; *illus. 16*

Columbus, Christopher, 14, 15, 23
commercial sailing ships, 2, 9, 13, 17, 131, 174
  iceboats as, 74
compromise hulls, 45
concave bottoms, 14, 15, 17; *illus. 16*
Corinthian Yacht Club (Marblehead, Mass.), 132
cotton sailcloth, 31, 94
  singed or varnished, 98, 101
Crowther, Locke, 145
cruising boats, 42, 63
  multihull vessels as, 102, 138, 143, 149
Cunningham, Charles and Lindsay, 134, 140
Cunningham hole, 119-22; *illus. 120*
Curry, Dr. Manfred, 97-98, 123
cutters, 44

Dacron for sailcloth, 101, 103
daggerboards, 71, 147
Daschew, Steve, 133
deadrise, 25, 33
deBisschop, Eric, 140, 141
deck layout of hardware and lines, 71
Defender (racing yacht), 53, 56
delamination of fiberglass hulls, 146
depressurization, 92, 103, 110
Deuce I, II, and *III* (stern-steering Class A iceboats), 98-99
development class rules for racing boats, 70, 71
  for iceboats, 84
diamonds, 61-63
Dilemma (fin keel racing yacht), 50-52, 58, 69, 130; *illus. 51*
dinghies, racing, 56, 97, 134, 139
  planing, 171
displacement, 32, 52, 127, 135, 137-38, 156, 173
DN iceboats, 84-87, 105; *illus. 86*
Dominion (catamaran), 132
double-luff rotating mast, *illus. 107*
drag, 3n., 167
drawings for shipbuilding, 44, 53
drop keel, 33
Duggan, G. Herrick, 131-32
Dutch shipping, 21, 25, 35
  iceboats in, 74; *illus. 75*

"E Skeeters" or "E boats" (iceboats), 84, 99 *and n.*, 101; *illus. 86*
effort, center of (CE), 4-5n., 78, 80, 91, 147; *illus. 8, 77, 79, 81, 83*
Egyptian ships, ancient, 2, 4-7, 91
eddies, undesirability of, 90, 91, 92, 105, 112, 122, 124, 153; *illus. 93, 107*
Elmina (schooner), *illus. 46*
Enterprise (racing yacht with Park Avenue boom), 126
epoxy saturation, 172

fabrics for sailcloth, 3, 31, 94, 101

false wind, 150-53, 157; *illus. 153*
fiberglass sandwich hulls, 145-46
fin-keel boats, 50-52, 130; *illus. 51, 58*
fins for lateral resistance, 17, 163
First World Multihull Championship, 144
flat bottoms, 37-38, 39, 143; *illus. 40, 136*
flicker, 80, 82
fluid flow, 32, 33, 35, 50, 135, 137, 143, 145
fore-and-aft rig, 17, 25, 28, 38, 44n.
fore-and-aft spritsails, 9-11, 21, 92, 94; *illus. 10*
  on iceboats, 76
forestay sail, 21, 74; *illus. 63*
freeboard, 24, 68, 138

gaff rig, 17, 21, 59, 66, 71, 74, 124, 131; *illus. 29*
  mainsail on iceboats, 76; *illus. 77*
gaffs, 28
Gardner, William, 44, 47, 48, 94
Gemini (catamaran), 135
Genoa jibs, 98, 103, 105, 172
Gerritt, Norm, 84
Gloriana (racing yacht), 48-50, 64; *illus. 49*
going downwind, 122
going to weather, 119, 122
Gougeon, Jan, 84
Gougeon, Meade, 103, 124, 160
Gougeon Brothers Company, 161, 172
gravity, center of (CG), 26, 35, 39, 56, 130, 149, 164; *illus, 40, 128*
Great Lakes, sailing on, 33, 69-70
  iceboating on, 82
Greece, ancient, shipping in, 2, 7

half-diamonds, 63
halyards, 19, 21, 26, 98
hardware, rigging, 26, 68, 71, 101, 172
Hearst International trophy, 99
hermaphrodite brig, *illus. 29*
Herreshoff, John, 52
Herreshoff, Nathanael G., 31, 44, 47, 48-53, 61, 69, 78, 94, 130, 131, 133-34
hike in iceboating, 80
hiking boards, 56
homespun fabric for sailcloth, 94
hoops, attaching sail by, 61; *illus. 60*
Hubbard, Dave and Jerry, 103
Hudson River Ice Yacht Club, 78
Hudson River type of iceboats, 76, 98; *illus. 78*
hull construction and shapes, 31-33, 68, 101, 102, 134-35, 145-46
  ancient Egyptian, 5-7
  Renaissance, 14-17
  evolution of, 14-15, 17; *illus. 16*
  Herreshoff's, 53
  of multihulls, 135-38, 141-43; *illus. 136*
hull speed, 30 *and n.*, 31, 172
hydrofoils, 141-42

iceboats, 71, Chap. VI *passim*, 98, 102, 103, 105, 119, 123, 153, 157-60, 169, 170, 171; *illus. 75, 77, 79, 81, 83, 85, 86*
Ice Yacht Challenge Pennant of America, 78
Icicle (stern-steering iceboat), 78, 98
Imperial Yacht Club (Kiev, Russia), 132
International Catamaran Development Class C, 102, 160, 169
International DN Ice Yacht Racing Association, 84
International Offshore Rule, 70

jibing, 11 *and n.*
jibs, 21, 76, 98, 124, 134, 156, 172
  overlapping (Genoa), 98, 103, 105, 172
Joy brothers, 82
jumper stays, 59, 61, 118; *illus. 62*
jumper strut, 61; *illus. 62*
junks of China, 15, 19; *illus. 20*

Kamiloa (catamaran), 140, 141
keelboats, modern, 42, 47, 71, 171
keels, 14, 33, 47
  in ancient shipbuilding, 7
Kelsall, Derek, 146
kicking strap, 119
"kit boat," 133
Kumalai, Alfred, 141

ladder-type foils, 164-67; *illus. 165*
lapstrake hulls, 7
lateen rig, 11-13, 15, 17, 21; *illus. 12*
  on iceboats, 80; *illus. 83*
lateral resistance, 15, 19, 31, 33, 74, 154
  center of (CLR), 4-5*n.*, 76, 91, 147; *illus. 8, 18, 46, 77, 81, 85*
  retractable, *illus. 34*
leading edge of sail, 61, 94, 115
leeboards, 35, 74; *illus. 34*
leech line, 122; *illus. 121*
leech of the sail, 59
lee helm, 3-4, 5*n.*, 9
leeway, 4, 33, 141, 143, 163
length, overall, in rating rules, 70
length-to-beam ratios in multihulls, 137
lift, 143, 167
Lindbergh, Charles A., 98
linen for sailcloth, 31, 76
Liris (racing yacht), 47; *illus. 46*
"Little America's Cup," 103, 146
Lodestar (trimaran), 144
Lodge, Joseph B., 84, 98, 99
low-profile hulls, uncapsizable, 38; *illus. 41*
luff of the sail, 61, 94
luffing of sail (fluttering), 94, 153
lug sail, slatted, 19, 21, 134; *illus. 20*
lug topsail, 19

mainsail, 7, 9, 11, 102, 103, 113, 134
Manu Kai ("*Sea Bird*") (catamaran),

141; *illus. 136*
Marblehead Race Week, 132
marine cordage, synthetic fiber, 101
marks (buoys) for racing, 68, 71
Marconi rig, 21, 28, 59, 66, 71, 95-97, 113, 118, 147, 153, 154, 157; *illus. 63, 96, 107*
mast load, 63-66, 78, 80, 82; *illus. 64, 81, 83, 85*
mast placement, principles of, 2-5, 9-11
  in iceboats, 78; *illus. 79, 81*
masthead jibs, 71, 172
masts, 9, 17, 25, 28, 102
  buckling, danger of, 63
  hollow, 63-66, 98; *illus. 65*
  metal, 66
  streamlined, 66, 98, 105; *illus. 107*
  A-frame for, 80; *illus. 83*
  as leading edge of airfoil, 94, 95, 113
  rotating, 98
  wing and rotating wing, 99, 101, 103, 105, 113, 122-23; *illus. 100, 107*
  box-spar, *illus. 107*
  bending, 115
  on multihull vessels, 147, 149
Mayflower, 24
measurement in racing, 68, 69
Mediterranean, development of shipping on, 4, 7-11, 13
Merritt, Charles and William, 80
Meyer, Starke, 82
Middle Ages, shipping in, 11-14, 21
Mischief (iron sloop), 44
models for shipbuilding, 44, 53
Morgan, Commodore E. D., 48
multihull vessels, 17, 102, 108, Chap. IX *passim*
multiple shrouds, 59; *illus. 62*
multiple stays, 59-63

navies, sailing, history of, 2, 13, 24
Newick, Dick, 147, 149
New Jersey type of iceboats, 80, 82; *illus. 83*
Newport 30's (one-design class racing yachts), 52
New York Yacht Club, 44, 48, 131
Nicol, Headley, 145
Nile River Valley, first use of sail in, 2, 4
Nimble (trimaran), 143-44
Niña (square-rigged caravel), 15-17
North American Multihull Championships, 102, 103, 160
Northmen, ships of the, 14, 15
nuclear power for ships, 174
Nugget (trimaran), 145
nylon for sailcloth, 101, 122

Ocelot (catamaran), 135
one-design classes, 71
  of scows, 58
  racing boats, 70
  catamarans, 70

iceboats, 84; *illus. 86*
One Hundred Guineas Cup, 43-44 ·
One-of-a-kind regattas, 133 *and n.,* 160
Ottking, Peter and Phil, 102, 103
outhaul, 113, 118, 122, 124; *illus. 114*
outrigging hulls, 145, 147

Pacific Multihull Association's World
     Championships, 1971, 133
Park Avenue boom, 126
Patterson, George, 103
Petty, Sir William, 130, 140
Pinta (square-rigged caravel), 15
Piver, Arthur, 143-45, 146
Plainview (foil-borne vessel), 164
planing, 132, 139, 143
planing hulls, 14, 32, 139
planked hulls, 7
plastics for hulls, 101, 171
plywood, waterproof sheet, for hulls, 101,
     133, 135, 140, 141, 144, 172
Polynesian canoes, 13, 17, 30*n.,* 130, 140
polyvinyl chloride foam, 146
Poughkeepsie Ice Yacht Club, 78
Preussen (5-masted square-rigger), 17
proas, 130, 147-49; *illus. 148*
"profile sail," 99
Prout, Roland and Francis, 134, 140
Puritan (compromise hull sloop), 45; *il-*
     lus. 46

racing, 3, 30, 45, 106
     rules of, 67-72, 173
     international iceboat championship, 84
racing sailboats, 42, 63, 67-72 *passim,* 106
     dinghies and small sailboats, 56, 59, 97,
          134, 139
     scows, 58
     multihull vessels, 103
     See also America's Cup defenders
rating rules, 69-70, 172
reaching, 68, 154-56; *illus. 155*
"ready-to-sail" boats, 102
real wind, 151, 157
reefing, 11, 19, 108, 140
reefing ties, 21
Renaissance, refinement of sailing ships
     during, 14
resin glues in boatbuilding, 133
Resolute, 47
Richard Peck (steamship), 44
ride, smoothness of, in multihulls, 143,
     145
     in hydrofoils, 169
rigging, 30, 31, 53, 71, 173
     on multihull vessels, 150
righting a capsized catamaran, 139-40
righting arm, 38 *and n.*
righting moment, 31-32
roach of the sail, 97, 99*n.,* 102
Robert Scott, 78
Roman ships, ancient, 7-11, 92; *illus. 8,*
     10

Roosevelt, John E., 78, 98
rotating streamlined mast, 102, 105, 108,
     118, 173; *illus. 107*
round bottoms, 14, 15, 37, 42, 135, 137,
     143, 145; *illus. 16, 136*
rowboats, 37-38, 39, 42; *illus. 40*
rudders, 3*n.,* 52, 58, 131, 134, 163
     in ancient ships, 2, 9
     mounted over stern, 15, 19
     steering without, 17-19; *illus. 18*
     over-the-side design, 19
     running (with the wind), 25, 26, 68, 156-
          60; *illus. 155*

safety in iceboats, 74
     in multihulls, 139-40, 144
sail area, 172
     in rating rules, 70, 71
Sailfish, Alcort's, 11
sailing hydrofoil craft, 167-70
sail handling, 140, 142
     on multihulls, 150
sail plan, 4, 5*n.,* 7, 30, 47, 50, 106
     on iceboats, 78
sails, design and cut of, 31, 71, 97
     use of wind by, analyzed, 90-91 *ff.; il-*
          lus. 93
     stowing, 108
     loose-foot, 124
sail track, 59-61, 63, 94, 123; *illus. 60*
sandbaggers, 55, 58
schooners, 28, 30, 33, 39, 44, 47; *illus. 29*
     definition of, 25
     colonial American, 43, 127
scows, 30*n.,* 56-58, 68, 69, 108; *illus. 57*
     classes of, 58, 101, 160
     one-design, 131-32
Sealion, 103
Seawanhaka Cup, 131, 132
self-stabilizing foils, 164-67; *illus. 165,*
     166
sewing methods in sailmaking, 31, 94,
     113, 122
shear, problem of, in sandwich-core hulls,
     146
Shearwater (catamaran), 134, 137; *illus.*
     136
sheets, 5, 9, 11, 21, 119, 140; *illus. 6*
Shields, Robert, 103
shrouds, 98, 108, 112, 118, 156
side-bending masts, 115-18, 119; *illus. 117*
Smith, A. Cary, 44-45, 48, 94
smuggling, effect on ship design of, 24-25
Snipe, 71
sloop rig, 132
     on iceboats, 80
sloops, 11, 21, 25, 28, 33, 44 *and n.,* 45,
     156; *illus. 29*
     gaff-rigged, 71
     daggerboard, 71
     flat-bottomed, as iceboat, 74
"slot effect," 103-5; *illus. 104*
spade rudder, 52, 71

spars, 28, 63, 95, 119
  box, 66
  See also masts
speed under sail, 1-2, 23-25, 74, 99, 102, 127
  on iceboats, 76, 84, 105n.
  in catamarans, 130, 133, 139, 149
  in trimarans, 144
  in hydrofoils, 170
spinnakers, 91-92, 113, 122, 156, 160, 173; *illus. 95*
Spirit of St. Louis (plane), 98
spreaders, 61; *illus. 62*
Sprinter, 103
square-riggers, 11, 15, 17, 24, 25, 26, 38, 92, 106, 127
  Egyptian, 2, 4-7
  19th century, 5
  control lines on, *illus. 6*
  Roman, 9
stability in sailing vessels, 38, 45n., 137; *illus. 40, 41*
  of catamarans, 130, 133; *illus. 128*
  of trimarans; *illus. 129*
"stall speed," 112
standing rigging, 28, 59-63, 101; *illus. 62*
Star, 71
staysails, 17, 21, 30
steam-driven vessels, 44, 48
steel, for hulls, 45
  tubular, for masts, 66
steering, 31
  without a rudder, 17-19; *illus. 18*
  geared, 39
  rope-tackle mechanisms for, 39
steering oars, 2, 17
Steers, George, 44
stern-steering on iceboats, 76, 98; *illus. 77, 79*
stiffness of hull, 33 *and n.*, 37-38
Stiletto (trimaran), 144
streamlined mast, 66, 98, 105; *illus. 107*
Stuart Cup trophy, 99
studding sails, 30
submersible outrigging hulls, 145
Sunfish, Alcort's, 11
swamping, dangers of, 68

tacking, 11, 19, 21
  downwind, 157-60; *illus. 159*
Tchetchet, Victor, 132-33, 135, 143
T-foils, 167; *illus. 168*
teeter-totter problem in iceboats, 78, 80; *illus. 81*
tenderness of hull, 33n., 42
tiller on iceboats, 76
"time on distance" method of rating, 70
"time on time" method of rating, 69
topsail, 7, 9

Toria (trimaran), 146
trailing edge of sail, 97, 115, 119
Trans-Atlantic Single Handers' Race, 144, 146, 147
trapezes, 56
trimarans, 30n., 102, 127, 130, 132-33, 135, 143-46, 171, 173; *illus. 128, 158*
T-shaped frame for iceboats, 76; *illus. 77, 85*
turning radius, short, in racing boats, 68
  in iceboats, 84

uni-rig (single-sail rig), 102-5
  disadvantages of, 106
Urie, Tom, 146

Valkyrie II (racing yacht), 52
Vanitie (racing yacht), 47
Vasa (square-rigged galleon), 26-28
V foils, 164; *illus. 166, 167*
Victor T (trimaran), 160
Vigilant (bronze bottom racing yacht), 52
Vikings, 14
Vindex (62-ft. cutter, iron yacht), 44
Volunteer (steel hull racing yacht), 45
Vooremaa, Eindel, 84
V-shaped bottoms, 25, 135, 145; *illus. 136*

warships, 1-2, 21, 24, 26, 38
Wasp (racing yacht), 52
waterline, relation of CG to, 26
waterline length, 14-15, 50, 69, 70, 137
waterline width, 137
weather helm, 3n., 5n., 76
weight aloft, reducing, 94, 127, 156
weight distribution, 26, 63-66, 80; *illus. 27*
  in multihull vessels, 150
weight factor in multihull design, 138-40
Westell, John, 146
wetted surface, 32, 33, 35, 38, 50, 127, 135, 138, 143, 145, 156, 167
wing mast, 99, 103, 105, 113; *illus. 100*
  rotating, 99, 101; *illus. 100, 107*
  disadvantages of, 106
  cambered, 122-23
wire rope, 17, 59, 63, 94
Wood, Gar, 98
Wright brothers, 164

Yacht Racing: The Aerodynamics of Sails (Curry), 97
yardarms (yards), 3, 25, 26, 80; *illus. 6, 11*
Yvonne Cat (catamaran), 134-35; *illus. 136*